Celebrate!

Healthy Entertaining
for Any Occasion

American Cancer Society
Health Promotions
1599 Clifton Road NE
Atlanta, Georgia 30329, USA

5 4 3 2 05 06 07 08 09

Printed in the United States of America
Designed by Jill Dible

Library of Congress Cataloging-in-Publication Data
Celebrate : healthy entertaining for any occasion / American Cancer Society.
p. cm.
Includes index.
ISBN 0-944235-18-2
1. Entertaining. 2. Cookery. I. American Cancer Society.

TX731 .C45 2001
642'.4--dc21

00-068929

Editor
Amy Brittain

Managing Editor
Gianna Marsella, MA

Book Publishing Manager
Candace Magee

Senior Lead, Content
Chuck Westbrook

Contributors/Consultants
Diana Priest
Anneke Smith
Trish Vignati, RD
Jodie Worrell

Editorial and Content Review
Terri Ades, MS, APRN, AOCN
Director of Cancer Information
American Cancer Society

Colleen Doyle, MS, RD
Director of Nutrition and Physical Activity
American Cancer Society

v (Why Celebrate Healthy?

v (How to Use this Book

1 (On the "Green" Golf Party

Basil and Tomato Bruschetta ■ Bloody Mary Mix ■ Spiced Chicken Breast ■ Lemon Barbecued Shrimp ■ Ginger Shredded Pork ■ Black Bean Cakes ■ Grilled Portabella Mushrooms ■ Mixed Greens with Assorted Vegetables, Fruits, Cheese, and Other Toppings ■ Homemade Lemon Dressing ■ Golf Ball Cookies

15 (Get Your Hands Dirty Garden Party

Chilled Asparagus with Horseradish-Dill Dipping Sauce ■ Raspberry Lemonade ■ Green Salad with Edible Flowers and Mustard Vinaigrette ■ Curried Chicken Salad ■ Marinated Artichoke and Potato Salad ■ Minted Melon Balls ■ Buttermilk Chocolate Drops

25 (Book Club Supper

Bibliophile Bread ■ Cliffhanger Cappuccino Coolers ■ Best-Seller Beet and Orange Salad ■ "Read" Pepper Soup with Sour Cream and Chives ■ Page-Turner Tuna Steaks with Ginger-Lime Crust ■ Novel New Potatoes and Sugar Snap Peas ■ Epilogue Praline-Apple Crisp

37 (Life is a Bowl of Cherries Celebration

Zucchini Bites ■ Crispy Shrimp Sensations ■ Cherry Limeade ■ Roast Turkey Breast with Sour Cherry Sauce ■ Crunchy Green Beans with Caramelized Onions ■ Brown Rice Pilaf ■ Cheery Cherry Parfaits

47 (Home on the Range Hoedown

Spicy Salsa Dip ■ Cowboy Cornbread ■ Root Beer Floats ■ Ranch Beans ■ Texas Dry-Rub Barbecue ■ Tri-Colored Jalapeño Slaw ■ Country Corn on the Cob ■ Round 'Em Up Oatmeal Carrot Bars

59 (Backyard Beach Barbecue

Red, Yellow, and Green Dip with Parmesan Pita Triangles ■ Seaside Punch ■ Skewered Shrimp, Chicken, and Pineapple with Honey-Orange Dipping Sauce ■ Red Bliss Potato Salad ■ Summer Fruit Salad with Poppy Seed Dressing ■ White Bean Salad ■ Lemon-Watermelon Slush

71 (Jamaican Jam

Jerk Shrimp with Berry Sauce ■ Montego Bay Papaya Punch ■ Coconut-Rum Salmon ■ Black Beans and Rice with Papaya and Red Onions ■ Baked Sweet Potato Wedges ■ Tropical Fruit Display ■ Banana Custard

83 (Salsa Party

Corn, Onion, Red Pepper, White Bean, and Cilantro Salsa ■ Pineapple, Peach, and Jalapeño Salsa ■ Sangría Blanca Punch ■ Mexican Chicken Salad ■ Black Bean–Filled Sweet Potato Biscuits with Queso Fresco ■ Jicama Slaw ■ Caribbean Rice and Beans ■ Key Lime Yogurt Pie

97 (Croquet Classic

Dilled Salmon Mousse ■ Mini Bean Croquettes with Tomato-Anchovy Dip ■ Summer Sparkler ■ Julienned Carrot and Celery Orzo ■ Seared Sesame Scallops with Avocado Sauce ■ Zucchini and Squash Tart ■ Summer Strawberry Shortcake

111 (Mount Olympus Greek Party
Heavenly Hummus ■ Cucumber Yogurt Dip ■ Nectar of the Gods ■ Lemon Spinach Soup ■ Greek Chicken with Tomatoes, Peppers, Olives, and Feta ■ Rice with Orzo and Mint ■ Greek Salad ■ Baklava with Fruit Compote

123 (Country Fair Canning Party
Blue Ribbon Sun-Dried Tomato Dip ■ Caramel Dipping Sauce ■ Mulled Punch ■ Farm-Fresh Deviled Eggs ■ Creamy Double-O Relish ■ Country Coleslaw ■ Harvest Ham Primavera ■ Blueberry Peach Crisp

137 (Pre-Hike Breakfast
Energizing Smoothie ■ Glorious Fruit Salad ■ Sparkling Sunset Citrus Spritzer ■ Rise 'n Shine English Muffins ■ Breakfast Burritos ■ Pumpkin Oat Muffins ■ Make-Your-Own-Cereal and On-the-Trail Mix

151 (Pumpkin-Carving Contest
Scary Spiced Popcorn ■ Turkey Sausage Bites with Sweet Hot Mustard Sauce ■ Hot Spiced Cider ■ Herb-Rubbed Pork Loin with Apricot-Pecan Stuffing ■ Spinach Soufflé ■ Harvest Rice ■ Pumpkin Mousse

163 (Game Night
Three Bean Creole Dip ■ Game Piece Grapes ■ Flip Juice ■ "Full" House Salad ■ Turkey Reuben Grilled Sandwiches ■ Eggplant Pizza ■ Scrumptious Carrot Cake

175 (Season's Greetings Holiday Affair
Spinach and Tomato Quesadilla Trees ■ Hot Cocoa ■ "Snow"-Dusted Fruit ■ Hearty Veggie Alphabet Soup ■ Confetti Beans and Rice ■ Festive Tuna Rollups ■ No-Bake Cookies

187 (Post-Holiday Blues Party
Green Chile Artichoke Dip ■ Blue Storm ■ Mixed Greens with Berry-Mustard Vinaigrette ■ "I Got the Blues" Chicken ■ Couscous with Almonds, Dried Blueberries, and Parmesan Cheese ■ Roasted Garlicky Potatoes ■ Lemon Cake with Brandied Blueberry Sauce ■

199 ("Souper" Bowl Bash
Kick-Off Crunch ■ Spiced Ginger Tea ■ Caesar Salad ■ Sideline Chicken Chili ■ Halfback Beef Burgundy Soup ■ Touchdown Tomato-Basil Soup ■ Fourth Quarter Chocolate Cheesecake

209 (This Must Be Love Valentine's Day Dinner
Polenta Hearts with Roasted Red Pepper and Olive Tapenade ■ Valentine Spritzers ■ Fruits of Love Salad with Blushed Vinaigrette ■ Rosemary Beef with Shallot Sauce ■ Buttermilk Garlic Mashed Potatoes ■ Ruby Red Beets with Fennel ■ Made in Heaven Strawberry Mousse

221 (Partito Italiano
Chianti-Grilled Mushrooms and Onions ■ Iced Cappuccino ■ Antipasto Salad ■ Crostini ■ Grilled Vegetables ■ Linguini with Tomato, Basil, and Capers ■ Dilled Carrots ■ Tiramisu

233 (Taste of Nations Dinner
Middle Eastern Baked Falafel ■ Iced Turkish Coffee ■ Artichoke Hearts Toscana ■ Indian Curried Carrot Soup ■ Hungarian Chicken ■ Greek Zucchini ■ Pears Hélène

245 (American Cancer Society Commitment to Nutrition and Health Promotion ■ American Cancer Society Guidelines for Diet, Nutrition, and Cancer Prevention ■ Resources ■ Conversion Tables for Cooking

251 (Index

Why Celebrate Healthy?

Most of us know that eating right and being physically active are important to maintaining good health. But we also know that getting together with friends for a meal or party often means being tempted by special-occasion treats and that planning for these special occasions frequently leaves little time for getting in a workout.

It can be easy and fun to incorporate a healthy diet and physical activity into your life—even on special occasions, when you may be most likely to overdo the fat and calories and least likely to be active. You can celebrate in style without taking a break from healthy eating or delicious food.

Healthy celebrations don't require more planning and effort. The themes in this book combine festive menus with creative yet manageable ideas for entertaining friends and family.

The activities suggested for each theme will help get you and your guests off the couch and into action—an important part of a healthy lifestyle. And the activities are sure to provide you and your guests with lasting memories of your get-together!

The delicious ideas you'll find in the American Cancer Society's *Celebrate! Healthy Entertaining for Any Occasion* will show you how easy it is to make a commitment to living healthy. And you aren't the only one who will benefit when you incorporate healthy habits into your entertaining routine—your friends and family will be inspired too.

You might be surprised to see that not all of the dishes here are low in fat and calories. Eating well doesn't mean every single thing you eat has to be "healthy." It means choosing healthy foods more frequently than less healthy foods, balancing the not-so-healthy foods with healthy foods, and eating reasonable portion sizes of the foods you choose.

How to Use This Book

The menus in *Celebrate! Healthy Entertaining for Any Occasion* are arranged by season and designed for eight people. Each theme includes a combination of appetizers, main dishes, side dishes, desserts, and beverages. For spring and summer we've offered lighter meals using the season's freshest ingredients and many reasons to enjoy the outdoors and milder weather. For your fall and winter special occasions, we've created cozy fare and ideas for taking advantage of crisp fall air and fireside get-togethers.

But you don't need to wait for a holiday or anniversary to use this book—we've given you plenty of reasons to celebrate. From a Backyard Beach Barbecue to a Book

Club Supper, you'll find lots of excuses to gather with friends. And the themes aren't just for Post-Holiday Blues or Pumpkin Carving. You can use them to create birthday brunches, weekend cookouts, movie nights, casual family get-togethers—you name it! Mix and match recipes from themes and adapt our ideas to develop healthy special occasion celebrations that appeal to you.

Nice weather allows for outdoor entertaining, and many of our themes suggest this as an option for celebrating. An outdoor party is an easy and casual way to gather friends for food and conversation. If your celebration involves spending a morning or afternoon outside, be sure to provide sunscreen for guests, and consider adding colorful umbrellas to your decor so guests enjoy good food and good company away from the sun.

- If you have room, set up drinks, appetizers, main dishes, and desserts on different tables to help the flow of guests.
- Set up any flowers, candles, and other decorations behind food so guests don't have to reach through an arrangement or a flame to serve themselves.
- Place plates at one end of the buffet table and napkins, forks, and knives at the other so guests can more easily hold their plates as they serve.
- After guests have served themselves, eat some of the food you've prepared. If the host doesn't eat, guests may feel uncomfortable.
- If you don't have enough chairs for everyone to sit down, clear enough empty surfaces so that guests may at least set down their drinks and plates.
- To keep yourself from overindulging, visit with guests away from the buffet table.

We've also suggested invitation, decoration, and "setting the scene" ideas so you can carry out each theme to its fullest if you wish. Come up with creative ideas of your own or simplify our ideas. A casual party doesn't require invitations, but invitations can help set the tone for the theme you're celebrating. Likewise, a simple flower arrangement or bowl of shined fruit and vegetables is a striking centerpiece and may be all that's necessary to decorate a table.

You may not want to serve every dish suggested for a theme, and you may want to mix and match among recipes from different themes. Send out invitations, decorate, and make each recipe for a dinner party, or make one appetizer and a dessert from a theme for a more impromptu gathering. Within any menu, consider providing both a dish that appeals to children and a meatless entree for vegetarian guests and others who are trying to limit their consumption of meat.

The guiding principle to using this book is this: Explore a theme to the extent that it's manageable and fun for you and your guests. Whether you're planning a simple dinner party, an intimate picnic, or an elaborate buffet, *Celebrate! Healthy Entertaining for Any Occasion* will help you plan, prepare, and serve in style...and in good health!

On the "Green" Golf Party

This golfing party features make-your-own salads with a variety of "greens" and toppings. Easy enough to offer after a day of golfing or attending a golf tournament, it's also fun to serve during televised golf events like the U.S. Open, the British Open, the PGA Championship, the Masters, the Ryder Cup, or the LPGA Championship.

menu for 8

- Basil and Tomato Bruschetta
- Bloody Mary Mix
- Spiced Chicken Breast
- Lemon Barbecued Shrimp
- Ginger Shredded Pork
- Black Bean Cakes
- Grilled Portabella Mushrooms
- Mixed Greens with Assorted Vegetables, Fruits, Cheese, and Other Toppings
- Homemade Lemon Dressing
- Golf Ball Cookies

Invitations

- To make your own invitations, cut green construction paper into the shape of a golf hole. Cut a "hole" from black construction paper or use a black marker to draw a black circle. Glue the paper on a piece of card stock. Create a flag made from a wooden skewer and triangular piece of paper and glue onto the hole. Write party information on the front or back.

- To save time, purchase golf-themed invitations from a stationery store.

Decorations

- Cover the buffet table with a green cloth (or if you're *really* creative, cover it with AstroTurf welcome mats set side by side). If you're holding the party outside and feel like being ambitious, consider using real sod as table covering. It's available in small pieces at garden centers.

- Use black or clear bowls to hold toppings for salad. Use a large bowl for mixed greens and elevate it on a pedestal covered with green cloth or AstroTurf.

- Consider labeling food items with flags made with dowels and glued-on paper flags.

- Serve the Golf Ball Cookies on green coconut "grass."

Activity

- Set up a putting green in the backyard, spare room, or basement. Give prizes for holes in one, longest putt, fanciest putt, etc. If you're holding a tough tournament, require guests to putt for their supper—only let them eat after everyone has gotten the ball into the hole.

Setting the Scene

- Show a golf tournament on TV or play soft classical music—you don't want to distract the golfers! Or play *Greatest Hits* by the jazz group Golf. Here are some ideas for classical background music:

  Messe de Pauvres by Erik Satie
  Moonlight: Night Moods by Ludwig von Beethoven
  Music of Bill Evans by the Kronos Quartet

increase your physical activity

Golfing can be great exercise, especially if you walk the course and carry your clubs.

Basil and Tomato Bruschetta

Rather than searching for perfectly ripe tomatoes, use quality canned tomatoes. They're the key to this year-round appetizer. Use less olive oil if you want to cut the calories in this appetizer.

2 28-ounce cans peeled whole tomatoes, drained, halved, and seeded
1/2 to 2/3 cup extra-virgin olive oil
14 large fresh basil leaves, torn
1 4-inch branch fresh rosemary
1/2 medium red onion, diced
5 large garlic cloves, chopped
Dash of salt
Dash of pepper
French bread loaf, sliced and toasted

Preheat oven to 300°F.

Spread the tomatoes on a cookie sheet and sprinkle with olive oil, basil, rosemary, onion, garlic, salt, and pepper. Turn to coat with oil.

Bake 1 hour 45 minutes to 2 hours 15 minutes, basting and turning the tomatoes twice to prevent tomatoes and garlic from browning. Remove from oven when tomatoes are dark red.

Transfer tomatoes to a glass bowl and let sit at room temperature until cooled.

Serve tomato mixture on top of bruschetta slices.

Serves 8.

bruschetta

You can top toasted French bread with practically anything and serve it as an elegant appetizer or first course. Layer soft cheese with roasted garlic paste, sauté mushrooms with shallots and rosemary, chop grilled vegetables, or spread with hummus and top with parsley—anything goes.

APPROXIMATE PER SERVING: *212 calories; 12 grams of fat*

Bloody Mary Mix

Serve this zesty recipe over ice with a celery stalk and you've got a delicious nonalcoholic cocktail—as well as a serving of vegetables!

2 46-ounce cans tomato juice
1/2 cup lime juice
1/3 cup juice from bottled jalapeños
1/3 cup white vinegar
1/4 cup sugar
4 teaspoons prepared horseradish
1/2 teaspoon salt
1/2 teaspoon pepper
1/4 teaspoon garlic powder
8 celery stalks

Combine first nine ingredients in a 2-quart pitcher. Store covered in the refrigerator. Serve with celery stalks.

Makes approximately 12 cups.
Serves 8.

you say tomato...

Each serving of this bloody mary mix contains over 100 percent of the recommended daily allowance for vitamin C. When you're not in the mood for a spicy kick, drink plain tomato juice—it offers the same vitamin C benefits.

APPROXIMATE PER SERVING: *120 calories; 0 grams of fat*

Spiced Chicken Breast

4 skinless, boneless chicken breast halves
1/4 cup flour
1/4 teaspoon garlic salt
1/4 teaspoon paprika
Dash of dry mustard
Dash of cayenne pepper (optional)
1/2 teaspoon olive oil
Cooking spray

Dredge chicken in flour.

Mix together garlic salt, paprika, mustard, and cayenne pepper.

Heat olive oil in large nonstick skillet over medium heat. Place chicken, breast side down, on hot skillet and cook 4 minutes.

Sprinkle chicken with half of seasoning mixture and spray with cooking spray. Turn breasts over, season again, and allow to cook 3 minutes or until cooked through.

Allow to cool. Slice thinly for salad topping.

Serves 8 with salad.

pickin' chicken

Choosing a chicken breast without the skin cuts the fat in each serving of this dish from almost 9 grams to 4.

APPROXIMATE PER SERVING: *70 calories; 4 grams of fat*

Lemon Barbecued Shrimp

3-1/3 pounds large fresh shrimp, peeled and deveined
2/3 cup fresh lemon juice
2/3 cup reduced-fat Italian salad dressing
1/3 cup water
1/3 cup light soy sauce
1/4 cup fresh parsley, minced
1/4 cup onion, minced
2 teaspoons garlic, minced
2/3 teaspoon freshly ground pepper

Arrange shrimp in a large, shallow dish.

Combine lemon juice, salad dressing, water, soy sauce, parsley, onion, garlic, and pepper in a jar. Cover tightly and shake jar vigorously.

Pour mixture over shrimp, cover, and marinate for approximately 4 hours. Drain, reserving marinade.

Preheat broiler or grill. Thread shrimp onto skewers. Arrange skewers on broiler pan or grill and cook 5 to 6 inches from a medium heat source for 3 to 4 minutes on each side, basting frequently with reserved marinade.

Serves 8 with salad.

wooden skewers

To prevent wooden skewers from burning on the grill, first soak them in water for an hour or until thoroughly saturated.

APPROXIMATE PER SERVING: *176 calories; 3 grams of fat*

Ginger Shredded Pork

Meat:

3 lean, boneless 1-1/2-inch-thick pork loin chops, trimmed

1 teaspoon ground ginger

1 teaspoon garlic salt

1/4 cup white vinegar

Sauce:

1/4 cup white vinegar

2 tablespoons ground ginger

1 teaspoon garlic salt

Preheat oven to 350°F.

TO PREPARE PORK: Place pork in aluminum foil-lined baking dish. Add vinegar, ginger, and garlic salt. Wrap foil around pork tightly, keeping ginger and vinegar mixture in the foil packet. Bake on middle rack of oven for 45 minutes or until cooked through.

Remove from oven and set aside until cool to the touch. Shred pork into bite-sized pieces.

TO PREPARE SAUCE: In a small saucepan, heat vinegar, ginger, and salt until thickened, approximately 2 minutes.

Toss pork with sauce until evenly coated.

Serves 8 with salad.

ginger

If a recipe calls for dried ground ginger, do not substitute fresh ginger—the flavors of each form are very different. Dried ground ginger is indispensable for certain soups, curries, meats, and desserts such as gingerbread, pumpkin pie, and spiced cookies.

APPROXIMATE PER SERVING: *180 calories; 10 grams of fat*

Black Bean Cakes

Cooking spray
1/2 medium sweet red bell pepper, diced finely
1/2 medium onion, diced finely
1 large carrot, sliced into thin coins
1 15-ounce can black beans, rinsed and drained well, mashed slightly
1 4-ounce can green chiles, chopped, undrained
1/2 cup cooked barley
1 tablespoon Parmesan cheese
1/4 teaspoon garlic salt
Dash hot sauce, or to taste
1/2 cup seasoned breadcrumbs
2 eggs, beaten

Lightly spray a medium nonstick skillet with cooking spray.

Over medium-high heat, sauté red pepper, onion, and carrot until tender. Set aside.

In a large bowl, mix together beans, green chiles, barley, cheese, garlic salt, and hot sauce. Mix in breadcrumbs, sautéed vegetables, and eggs.

Form bean mixture into tablespoon-sized balls. Drop onto nonstick skillet that has been lightly sprayed with cooking spray and heated to medium-high heat. Flatten each ball into a cake with spatula.

Cook 1 minute per side or until crispy and brown.

Serves 8 with salad.

beans, beans, good for the heart

Canned beans are an easy way to add fiber, protein, and phytochemicals to your diet. Beans are excellent sources of many vitamins and minerals, protein, and fiber. They're especially rich in nutrients that may protect against cancer.

APPROXIMATE PER SERVING: *180 calories; 2 grams of fat*

Grilled Portabella Mushrooms

1 cup Marsala wine
2 teaspoons balsamic vinegar
1/2 teaspoon garlic salt
1/4 teaspoon pepper
4 large Portabella mushroom caps, quartered

Mix wine, vinegar, and seasonings together in a small bowl.

Place mushroom caps in a resealable plastic bag and pour in marinade. Seal and marinate at least 3 hours.

Grill on medium heat directly on grill until tender, approximately 4 minutes per side.

Serves 8 with salad.

mushrooms Mushroom caps are actually the fruit of the mushroom plant, similar to apples on an apple tree. Portabella mushrooms are mature cremini mushrooms.

APPROXIMATE PER SERVING: *60 calories; 0 grams of fat*

Mixed Greens
with Assorted Vegetables, Fruits, Cheese, and Other Toppings

MIXED GREENS—*offer a selection of the following: Romaine, iceberg, Boston, or red leaf lettuce.*

Wash and dry greens, then tear into bite-sized pieces to total 16 cups (serving size: 2 cups).

VEGETABLES—*offer a selection of the following: bell peppers, onions, mushrooms, tomatoes, sprouts, carrots, cabbage, cucumbers, artichoke hearts, and hearts of palm.*

Wash and slice red, green, and yellow bell peppers; red and white onions; and mushrooms. Wash grape tomatoes and sprouts. Shred carrots and purple cabbage. Peel and slice cucumbers. Chop canned artichoke hearts and hearts of palm.

FRUITS—*offer a selection of the following: strawberries, grapes, kiwi, dried fruit, mandarin oranges, and pineapple.*

Slice fresh strawberries and grapes. Peel and slice kiwi. Offer dried fruit and canned mandarin oranges and pineapple chunks as well.

CHEESE—*offer a selection of the following: Feta, blue cheese, Parmesan, mozzarella, and reduced-fat cheddar.*

OTHER—*offer a selection of the following: Pumpernickel croutons, olives, sunflower seeds, wheat germ, and granola.*

Calories and fat will vary depending on ingredients and serving size.

Homemade Lemon Dressing

Offer Homemade Lemon Dressing as well as other assorted purchased dressings, such as low-fat Oriental, herb vinaigrette, raspberry vinaigrette, and light ranch with the mixed greens and toppings. This dressing is also an excellent marinade for fish or chicken.

1/2 cup fresh lemon juice
1/4 cup fresh parsley, chopped (or 1 tablespoon dried parsley)
1/4 cup green onion tops or fresh chives, chopped
2 tablespoons olive oil
2 cloves garlic, minced

Combine lemon juice, parsley, green onion tops, olive oil, and garlic in a small bowl and mix well with a whisk.

Makes approximately 1 cup.
Serves 8.

squeezing lemons

Bring fresh citrus such as lemons, limes, and oranges to room temperature before squeezing them. Then roll the fruit on a flat surface while pressing down or microwave it for 30 seconds. This increases the amount of juice you'll be able squeeze.

APPROXIMATE PER SERVING: *45 calories; 2.5 grams of fat*

Golf Ball Cookies

When making these cookies, make sure the mixture is cool or it will not form into balls easily.

Golf balls:
3/4 cup dates, pitted, chopped finely
3/4 cup dried apricots, chopped finely
1/4 cup corn syrup
2 teaspoons butter
2 tablespoons canola oil
1/4 teaspoon salt
2 cups crisp rice cereal
1/2 cup powdered sugar

Golf green (optional):
1 14-ounce package flaked coconut
Green food coloring

Mix dates, apricots, corn syrup, butter, oil, and salt together in a medium saucepan and bring to boil over medium-high heat. Simmer 2 minutes, stirring constantly. Remove from heat and mix in cereal until completely coated.

Let sit until mixture is cool to touch. Shape mixture into golf ball-sized balls. Roll each in powdered sugar.

Mix flaked coconut with green food coloring. Sprinkle onto serving platter. Place golf balls (cookies) on top of coconut (golf green).

Makes 16 cookies.
Serves 8.

coconuts

The name "coconut" is a misnomer. The coconut isn't a nut; it's the largest seed known to exist. Coconuts are high in saturated fat and are good sources of potassium.

APPROXIMATE PER SERVING: *210 calories; 4.5 grams of fat*

NOTES

Get Your Hands Dirty Garden Party

Invite adults and kids to adopt a plot in a community garden, plant a traffic island, or help a new homeowner landscape the yard or put in spring annuals. Reward the group with a meal suited for hardworking gardeners.

This is especially great as a housewarming party. Ask guests to donate their time and labor as a housewarming gift, or ask everyone to bring a plant with them as well.

menu for 8

- Chilled Asparagus with Horseradish-Dill Dipping Sauce
- Raspberry Lemonade
- Green Salad with Edible Flowers and Mustard Vinaigrette
- Curried Chicken Salad
- Marinated Artichoke and Potato Salad
- Minted Melon Balls
- Buttermilk Chocolate Drops

Invitations

- Purchase seed packets. Write party details on pieces of card stock and glue a seed packet to each one. Take into consideration your party goal and decorate card stock with dried flowers, for example, or use markers to draw a colorful vegetable border.

- SAMPLE WORDING (BE SURE TO INCLUDE A RAIN DATE): Come work for your supper! Help the Smiths plant their spring garden and enjoy a restful dinner afterward. Wear your garden clothes and be ready to get your hands dirty with friends! Soil, seeds, and soap will be provided…just bring your willing hands and work gloves.

Decorations

- To welcome guests, prop a rake against the front door and attach either flowers or a sign directing people to the garden.

- Plan to eat outside, weather permitting. Cover the buffet table with a green tablecloth and add potted flowers or a planted window box for decoration. You can also glue seed packets to Popsicle sticks and put them in the potted plants. Galvanized watering cans are attractive vases for flowers.

- Arrange clean trowels and spades—using children's sand toys if you like—around the table as well. Consider winding a clean hose around the pots on the table.

- Line flowerpots and saucers with glass or plastic and use them to hold salads and melon. As an alternative to placing seed packets on Popsicle sticks as suggested above, write menu items on card stock and glue to Popsicle sticks, then use to label dishes. Or write menu items on white plastic plant labels.

- When preparing the Buttermilk Chocolate Drops, bake the full recipe and wrap half the cookies in small cellophane bags tied with colored ribbon. You can even place the cookie bags in small, inexpensive plastic flowerpots for guests to take home, and attach flowered thank-you tags.

Activities

- Plant flowers or vegetables in a community garden plot, a traffic island, or a homeowner's flowerbed. Make sure you've got all the materials you need for planting—plants, soil, fertilizer, a plan for the garden, tools, etc.

- Kids will have fun playing with "worms in dirt"—offer them gummy worms and crumbled low-fat chocolate cookies or cake in clean green plastic flowerpots. They can eat the worms when they're finished.

- Invite guests inside to clean themselves up after the day's work is through and enjoy looking over the garden while eating dinner.

Setting the Scene

- Play your favorite upbeat music on a portable stereo while you're working. Some possibilities:

  Live at the Apollo by Diana Ross and the Supremes
  Under the Table & Dreaming by Dave Matthews Band
  Hard Day's Night by the Beatles
  Graceland by Paul Simon
  Faith by George Michael

Chilled Asparagus with Horseradish-Dill Dipping Sauce

1 pound asparagus, tough ends removed
8 ounces light sour cream
2 teaspoons horseradish
3 tablespoons fresh dill, minced
1/4 teaspoon garlic, minced
1/2 teaspoon lemon juice
1 ripe avocado, mashed
2 teaspoons light mayonnaise

Boil water in a large saucepan. Blanch asparagus in boiling water for 3 to 5 minutes until bright green.

While asparagus is boiling, prepare a large bowl of ice water. When asparagus has boiled 3 to 5 minutes, remove from pan and plunge into ice water. Chill completely. Drain asparagus, dry, and wrap in dishtowel.

Store asparagus in refrigerator crisper until ready to serve.

Mix together sour cream, horseradish, dill, garlic, lemon juice, avocado, and mayonnaise. Chill until ready to serve.

Serves 8.

blanching (Also called parboiling, blanching means briefly submerging foods such as fruits and vegetables in boiling water, then in cold water. Blanching loosens skins, firms the tissue, and increases the color and flavor of the food before eating or freezing.

APPROXIMATE PER SERVING: *90 calories; 7 grams of fat*

Raspberry Lemonade

2 12-ounce cans frozen lemonade concentrate, thawed
2 10-ounce packages frozen sweetened raspberries, partially thawed
3 tablespoons sugar
2 liters club soda, chilled

In a blender, combine lemonade concentrate, raspberries, and sugar.

Cover and process until blended. Strain to remove seeds.

In a 1-gallon container, combine raspberry mixture and club soda. Serve over ice cubes.

Makes approximately 13 cups.
Serves 8.

vitamin C, please

A pitcher of this refreshing drink packs a vitamin C punch—420% of the recommended daily allowance.

APPROXIMATE PER SERVING: *250 calories; 0 grams of fat*

Green Salad with Edible Flowers and Mustard Vinaigrette

Edible flowers, purchased from specialty stores or supermarkets that carry gourmet produce, should be tightly wrapped and stored in the refrigerator up to a week.

Dressing:
1/3 cup fat-free Italian dressing
1/4 teaspoon Dijon mustard
1/4 teaspoon horseradish
1 tablespoon poppyseeds

Salad:
2 cups Bibb lettuce, washed and torn
2 cups radicchio lettuce, washed and torn
2 cups Romaine lettuce, washed and torn
1 yellow bell pepper, diced
2 Roma tomatoes, diced
1/2 cup canned artichoke hearts, drained and chopped
2 tablespoons raisins
2 tablespoons sunflower seeds
1/2 cup edible flowers, such as sweet roses or pansies, if available

Whisk together all dressing ingredients.

Just before serving, toss lettuce, pepper, tomatoes, and artichoke hearts with dressing in large bowl.

Top salad with raisins, sunflower seeds, and flowers.

Serves 8.

a rose by any other name would taste as sweet

• Edible flowers can be used as a garnish or as part of a food dish. Some popular edible flowers are: nasturtiums, which taste peppery; mild, onion-like chive blossoms; pansies and violas, with a flavor similar to grapes; and sweet roses. Many blooms from fruit trees are also edible. • To clean and dry lots of lettuce, wash the leaves thoroughly, then place them in a clean pillowcase. Close the pillowcase and toss it into the washing machine for about a minute on the spin cycle (without detergent or bleach!).

APPROXIMATE PER SERVING: *70 calories; 2 grams of fat*

Curried Chicken Salad

1 small onion, sliced thinly
4 boneless, skinless chicken breast halves
2 teaspoons curry powder, divided
1/4 teaspoon garlic salt
1/4 cup orange juice
1 15-ounce can mandarin oranges, drained well
4 scallions, chopped finely
1 cup golden raisins
2 tablespoons sweetened, flaked coconut, divided
1/4 cup light mayonnaise
24 whole-wheat crackers

Preheat oven to 400°F.

Scatter onion slices on the bottom of a medium baking dish. Place chicken in baking dish and sprinkle with curry and garlic salt. Pour orange juice around chicken.

Bake for 15 minutes or until cooked through. Cool, then cut into bite-sized pieces.

In a medium bowl, mix chicken, oranges, scallions, raisins, and 1 tablespoon of coconut. Stir in mayonnaise.

Transfer to serving bowl and top with remaining coconut. Serve with whole-wheat crackers.

Serves 8.

packed with vitamin C

A mandarin orange is a category of tangerine. It has a light orange color, with a mild, sweet flavor and few seeds. Citrus fruits like mandarin oranges contain vitamin C, an antioxidant, which stops free radicals from damaging cells. Vitamin C is thought by some to enhance the immune system by stimulating the activities of white blood cells and anticancer agents.

APPROXIMATE PER SERVING: *300 calories; 7 grams of fat*

Marinated Artichoke and Potato Salad

2 pounds small red potatoes, quartered
2 cups green beans, cut into 1/2-inch pieces (about 1/2 pound)
1 6-ounce bottle marinated artichoke hearts
2 tablespoons chopped, pitted Kalamata olives
2 tablespoons white wine vinegar
2 tablespoons fresh parsley, chopped
1/2 teaspoon salt
1/4 teaspoon black pepper

Place potatoes in a large saucepan and cover with water. Bring to a boil and cook 20 minutes or until very tender. Add beans and cook 2 minutes or until beans are crisp-tender. Drain potato and bean mixture.

Drain artichokes in a colander over a bowl, reserving 2 tablespoons of marinade. Chop artichokes. Add artichokes and olives to potato-bean mixture.

Combine reserved 2 tablespoons of artichoke marinade with vinegar, parsley, salt, and pepper.

Drizzle dressing over salad, tossing to coat. Cover and chill.

Serves 8.

artichoke artifacts

A thistle and a member of the sunflower family, the artichoke itself is a flower bud or immature flower head. Artichokes are good sources of potassium.

APPROXIMATE PER SERVING: *126 calories; 3.8 grams of fat*

Minted Melon Balls

2 cups watermelon, seedless or seeds removed
2 cups cantaloupe
2 cups honeydew melon
1/4 cup water
2 tablespoons sugar
2 teaspoons lime juice
3 tablespoons fresh mint, chopped finely

Scoop out watermelon, cantaloupe, and honeydew melon meat with a melon baller.

In a small saucepan over medium heat, bring water, sugar, and lime juice to a boil. Boil 2 minutes and remove from heat.

Cool completely.

Toss sugar mixture together with melon and mint.

Chill well.

Serves 8.

melons

All melons, generally considered to be fruits, are really vegetables. They are related to the cucumber and the gourd.

APPROXIMATE PER SERVING: *60 calories; 0 grams of fat*

Buttermilk Chocolate Drops

You may want to reward your friends by giving each guest a small bag of cookies (see Decoration ideas at the start of this section) to take home.

1 cup light brown sugar, packed
1/2 cup shortening
4 1-ounce squares unsweetened chocolate
1 egg
1 teaspoon vanilla extract
1-3/4 cups all-purpose flour
2 teaspoons baking powder
1/2 teaspoon baking soda
1/4 teaspoon salt
1/2 cup buttermilk

Preheat oven to 350°F.

Melt chocolate on low heat in top portion of a double boiler.

Cream brown sugar and shortening in a mixer bowl until light and fluffy. Add chocolate, egg, and vanilla, and mix well.

In a small bowl, combine flour, baking powder, baking soda, and salt, mixing lightly.

Add dry ingredients to creamed mixture alternately with buttermilk, mixing well after each addition.

Bake the full amount of batter and send treats home with guests as suggested above, or freeze half the dough for later use.

Drop dough by teaspoonfuls onto lightly greased cookie sheets or nonstick cookie sheets.

Bake for 12 to 15 minutes or until brown.

Half the recipe serves 8.

buttermilk gets the thumbs up!

Buttermilk is made from fresh pasteurized or ultra-pasteurized low-fat or skim milk, usually with nonfat dry milk solids added. Buttermilk is a relatively low-fat product—1 cup contains about 2 grams of fat (a cup of whole milk contains 8 grams of fat, and a cup of 1% milk contains 2.5 grams of fat).

APPROXIMATE PER SERVING: *54 calories; 3 grams of fat*

Book Club Supper

A book club is a great way for friends to get together over hors d'oeuvres or dinner to discuss literature and life. Here we've offered a buffet menu so guests can choose what to balance on their knee during the discussion.

As the host, you may want to choose the book—with or without input from the group—and schedule the party a few weeks in advance so guests have time to read it.

If you have regular book group meetings, you may need ever-changing menus. Begin by preparing the menus in this book. You may want to ask guests to help you serve a potluck and assign cooking homework to each. If you want to explore a book's theme, serve cuisine from the region where the action takes place.

menu for 8

- Bibliophile Bread
- Cliffhanger Cappuccino Coolers
- Best-Seller Beet and Orange Salad
- "Read" Pepper Soup with Sour Cream and Chives
- Page-Turner Tuna Steaks with Ginger-Lime Crust
- Novel New Potatoes and Sugar Snap Peas
- Epilogue Praline-Apple Crisp

Invitations

- Send homemade or purchased bookmarks as invitations, with party information on the back, or offer invitations related to theme of the book, such as a magnolia motif for *Gone with the Wind*, a whale for *Moby Dick*.

- You might want to include a favorable review of the book or a synopsis. If you're ambitious, create a folding "book jacket" invitation with the book title and party information on the front, actual book reviews printed on the back, and the book summary on the flaps.

Decorations

- Arrange stacks of books as a table centerpiece. Set up a stack of varied hardback titles or old leather books, if you have them, tied with pretty ribbons and flowers.

- When guests arrive, offer them each a bookmark with the name of a character from the book written on the back. Ask each guest to offer impressions of or insights into "their" character.

- If you're having a seated dinner, use bookmarks as place cards. Write or print a list of possible discussion questions on place mats to get the discussion jump-started.

- If you'll be holding regular meetings, use props relevant to the topic or genre to help you decorate. For a mystery book, for example, you might want to start by setting up low lighting and murder props from a costume shop.

- You may want to display a menu designed to resemble a page from a book.

Activity

- Discuss the book assigned, using questions you've developed to begin the conversation if you like. Talk about passages that impacted readers positively and negatively, characters' motives and challenges, plot twists, and anything else that people want to discuss.

- An activity that is sure to entertain the group is book-themed charades. Separate the group into teams and ask each team to write book titles on pieces of paper, fold them, and put them in a bowl for the other team to act out.

Setting the Scene

- Play music related to the theme of the book, if appropriate. For example:

  For a discussion of Frank McCourt's *Angela's Ashes*, play Celtic music:
  The Visit by Loreena McKennitt
  Chieftains 4 by the Chieftains
  Acoustic Music to Suit Most Occasions by the Deighton Family

  For a discussion of *Corelli's Mandolin* by Louis De Bernieres, play Italian folk music or mandolin music:
  Mandolins of Italy by Angelo Petisi
  Guccini Live Collection by Francesco Guccini

  Play African music in the background when discussing Barbara Kingsolver's *The Poisonwood Bible*:
  Zaire: Music of the Bena Luluwa by various artists
  Zaire: Musiques de L'Ancien Royaume Kub by various artists

- If the book was made into a movie and you're not a purist, play music from the movie soundtrack. Or watch the video and compare the book and movie, as you could with *To Kill a Mockingbird*, *Jane Eyre*, *Little Women*, and more.

Bibliophile Bread

This can easily be made the day before. Be sure to store it in an airtight container so it remains fresh.

6 cups unbleached or bread flour, divided
1/4 cup fresh parsley, finely chopped
2 packages dry rapid rise yeast
2 tablespoons fresh basil, chopped
2 tablespoons fresh chives, finely chopped
2 teaspoons fresh rosemary, finely chopped
2 teaspoons salt
2-1/4 cups hot water (120°F to 130°F)
Cooking spray

Place 5 cups of flour into a food processor container fitted with a plastic dough blade. Add parsley, yeast, basil, chives, rosemary, and salt. Process, gradually adding water. Add enough of the remaining 1 cup of flour to make a non-sticky dough that loosens from sides of container.

Dust a board lightly with flour, place dough on board, and turn dough, kneading until smooth and elastic.

Lightly coat large bowl with cooking spray and dust lightly with flour. Place dough in bowl and set in a warm, draft-free place for 30 to 40 minutes or until doubled in bulk.

Punch dough down, knead briefly, and return to bowl. Let rise for 30 minutes or until doubled in bulk.

for crispy crusts

To produce loaves with a crisp crust, place 2 ice cubes in the bottom of the oven to create steam.

Preheat oven to 400°F.

Dust a board lightly with flour, place dough on board, and turn the dough, kneading several times. Divide into 2 portions. Shape each into a 15-inch-long loaf.

Place loaves side by side on an ungreased baking sheet. Cover with a cotton cloth and let rise for 15 minutes or until risen slightly but not doubled in bulk. With a sharp blade, cut 3 diagonal parallel slashes in the top of each loaf. Place baking sheet on bottom rack of the oven. Bake 45 minutes or until golden brown.

Makes 2 loaves.
Serves 8.

herbs—dried or fresh?

Dried herbs have a stronger, more concentrated flavor than fresh herbs, so that less is needed in the same recipe. However, dried herbs quickly lose their intensity and should not be stored longer than 6 months. To maintain your dried herbs' flavor, store them in an airtight storage container.

APPROXIMATE PER SERVING: *77 calories; 0.2 grams of fat*

Cliffhanger Cappuccino Coolers

Brew the coffee at double strength (twice as many grounds for the same amount of water) to prevent this drink from being watered down by the ice.

4 cups strong coffee or espresso, prepared
4 cups light vanilla ice cream
2 cups fat-free milk
2 cups fat-free whipped topping
4 dashes unsweetened cocoa
20 ice cubes
8 dashes cinnamon

Combine coffee, ice cream, milk, whipped topping, and cocoa in a blender, blending until smooth. Add ice cubes one at a time and blend until all ice is crushed.

Pour into coffee cups or small glasses and sprinkle with cinnamon.

Makes approximately 8 cups.
Serves 8.

java jargon

After Secretary of the Navy Josephus Daniels abolished alcohol on naval ships in 1913, the men referred to coffee—the next-strongest drink on board—as a "cup of joe." • The name "java" comes from the island of Java, a major producer of coffee. • The darker the roast, the less caffeine there is in the beans. Roasting burns away the caffeine along with the rest of the bean.

APPROXIMATE PER SERVING: *190 calories; 3 grams of fat*

Best-Seller Beet and Orange Salad

This dish is not only vibrant in color. It's also healthful and delicious. You may be surprised how good beets can taste!

12 beets (about 3 pounds)
6 3-inch orange rind strips
1 cup fresh orange juice
1/4 cup cider vinegar
1/2 cup sliced green onions
1/4 cup packed brown sugar
1/4 cup grated orange rind
1/4 cup Dijon mustard
8 cups gourmet salad greens
Orange rind strips for garnish

Clean beets with a scrub brush. Remove roots and stems. Peel beets and cut in half lengthwise, then cut into 1/4-inch-thick slices.

Place beets, orange rind strips, orange juice, and vinegar in a 6-quart pressure cooker. Close the lid securely and bring to high pressure over high heat, about 4 minutes. Maintain high pressure while decreasing the heat to medium or medium-high. Cook for 3 minutes.

Remove from heat and place pressure cooker under cold running water.

Reserve 1 cup of cooking liquid from the pressure cooker. Drain the beets. Discard the 6 orange rind strips.

Combine the reserved cooking liquid, beets, onions, sugar, grated orange rind, and mustard in a bowl; toss gently.

Place 1 cup of greens on each plate; top with beet mixture.

Garnish with additional orange rind strips, if desired.

Serves 8.

no more beet stains

Beets leave stains on hands, linens, and countertops. To prevent stains, wear disposable rubber gloves and place wax paper on your cutting board before preparing beets. Just dispose of the gloves and wax paper when you're done.

APPROXIMATE PER SERVING: *142 calories; 0.6 grams of fat*

"Read" Pepper Soup with Sour Cream and Chives

Serve this colorful soup in small teacups or bowls.

4 medium potatoes, peeled, cut into eighths
1/2 teaspoon salt
6 cloves garlic, peeled
2 large red bell peppers, cut into 3/4-inch rings
2 tablespoons light cream cheese
1 cup 1% milk
1/2 cup stewed tomatoes, drained and chopped into 1-inch pieces
4 dashes hot pepper sauce
1/4 cup light sour cream
1/4 cup chives, chopped

In a medium saucepan, bring potatoes, salt, and garlic to a boil. Reduce to simmer. Simmer 10 minutes, then drain well.

Heat burner or grill to high heat and place pepper rings *directly on surface.* Cook for 1 minute per side until tender (it's fine to develop black grill marks). Remove from heat and cool.

In a food processor, process potato mixture, peppers, and cream cheese until smooth.

Transfer mixture back to saucepan and stir in milk, tomatoes, and hot pepper sauce. Heat to a gentle boil, then remove from heat.

Serve in small bowls or cups. Garnish with a dollop of sour cream and a sprinkle of chives.

Makes approximately 4 cups.
Serves 8.

pepper particulars

Red bell peppers are simply vine-ripened green bell peppers. Because they've ripened longer, they tend to be sweeter than most. One serving of bell peppers packs a powerful Vitamin C punch—150% of your recommended daily allowance.

APPROXIMATE PER SERVING: *120 calories; 2 grams of fat*

Page-Turner Tuna Steaks with Ginger-Lime Crust

Steaks:
1/2 teaspoon olive oil
1/2 cup plain bread crumbs
1 teaspoon lime juice
1 teaspoon ginger
1 teaspoon brown sugar
1 teaspoon minced garlic
8 4-ounce tuna steaks

Sauce:
4 teaspoons lime juice
4 teaspoons soy sauce
1 teaspoon ginger
1/2 teaspoon garlic salt
2 tablespoons plus 2 teaspoons brown sugar, divided

Heat broiler (place rack on second rung from top).

Rub large heavy nonstick baking pan with olive oil.

Mix bread crumbs, lime juice, ginger, brown sugar, and garlic. Press onto both sides of tuna steaks to form crust.

Place tuna in pan and broil 5 minutes. Turn tuna and broil an additional 3 minutes.

Reduce oven to 350°F and cook 2 to 3 minutes more, until center is cooked through.

Whisk together sauce ingredients. Place tuna on serving dish, and pour sauce over each steak.

Serves 8.

tuna tidbit

While tuna is low in fat, research shows that the type of fat in Albacore tuna, known as omega-3 fatty acids, may be beneficial for lowering heart disease risk. • Most varieties of fresh tuna are available in late spring to early fall. Frozen tuna, in steaks or fillets, is available year-round. Extremely versatile in the kitchen, tuna can be baked, broiled, grilled, or fried.

APPROXIMATE PER SERVING: *210 calories; 6 grams of fat*

Novel New Potatoes and Sugar Snap Peas

Sugar snap peas should only be cooked for a short time so they retain their crisp texture.

24 small red new potatoes, scrubbed
2 small onions, sliced thinly
4 teaspoons olive oil
4 cups sugar snap peas, washed and strings removed
1/8 teaspoon salt
1/8 teaspoon pepper

Place potatoes in a medium saucepan, cover with water, and bring to a boil. Cook for 10 to 15 minutes until tender. Remove from heat, drain, and set aside.

In the same saucepan, sauté onion in oil until tender. Add snap peas and sauté until crisp-tender. Return potatoes to pan and stir together with onions and peas.

Season with salt and pepper.

Serves 8.

sweet pea

Sugar snap peas are also called sweet peas. Both the pod and pea are edible and can be eaten raw. When cooking sugar snap peas, sauté them only briefly so they remain crisp.

APPROXIMATE PER SERVING: *330 calories; 2.5 grams of fat*

Epilogue Praline-Apple Crisp

1 cup dark corn syrup
1/4 cup brown sugar, divided
2 tablespoons butter
1/2 teaspoon salt
20 square graham crackers, crushed
1/4 cup pecans, chopped
Cooking spray
8 large unpeeled Granny Smith apples, sliced
2 teaspoons lemon juice
2 teaspoons cinnamon
1 package fat-free ice cream or fat-free whipped topping (optional)

Preheat oven to 425°F.

In a medium saucepan, bring corn syrup, 2 tablespoons of brown sugar, butter, and salt to a boil over medium-high heat. Boil 3 minutes until mixture foams up, stirring constantly.

Stir in graham crackers and nuts; cool.

Lightly coat a small baking dish with cooking spray and press graham cracker mixture into dish to form a crust (this will be the topping).

In a separate bowl, toss apples with lemon juice, cinnamon, and 2 remaining tablespoons of brown sugar.

Spoon apples over graham cracker crust and bake for 10 minutes at 425°F. Reduce heat to 350°F and bake for an additional 20 minutes.

Remove from oven and cool.

Spoon crisp, crust side up, into bowls.

Serve with fat-free ice cream or whipped topping.

Serves 8.

sweet treat

Praline is a brittle candy made of nuts and caramelized sugar. It can be eaten straight, ground and used as a filling or dessert ingredient, or sprinkled on desserts.

APPROXIMATE PER SERVING: *480 calories; 7 grams of fat*

NOTES

Life is a Bowl of Cherries Celebration

Take the cheery old saying "life is a bowl of cherries" to heart when celebrating a graduation, anniversary, new baby, or other happy event. This cherry-themed menu is really appropriate anytime a celebration is in order, whether the occasion is the first blooms in your summer garden or a friend's big promotion.

menu for 8

- Zucchini Bites
- Crispy Shrimp Sensations
- Cherry Limeade
- Roast Turkey Breast with Sour Cherry Sauce
- Crunchy Green Beans with Caramelized Onions
- Brown Rice Pilaf
- Cheery Cherry Parfaits

Invitations

- Cut card stock in the shape of a cherry and stem and color it red and green, or hand-stamp or purchase cherry-themed invitations. Write party information on the back.
- SAMPLE WORDING: Life is a Bowl of Cherries… • Joe's landed the job of a lifetime • Lela's having a baby • Dad's celebrating his 60th birthday • Mary's retiring after 30 years teaching • Jon's graduating from college • Mark and Jackie bought a new house • Join us for dinner to celebrate!

Decorations

- Cherries themselves are striking enough to be gorgeous decorations on their own. For a simple centerpiece, fill a large glass bowl with fresh (or artificial) cherries.
- Arrange white votive candles on a simple white or red tablecloth, or hand-stamp cherries in fabric paint on a white tablecloth.
- Chocolate-covered cherries are commercially available and make beautiful party favors. Wrap some in cellophane bags and tie with red ribbons to send home with guests.

Activity

- Celebrate in the tradition of national and regional cherry festivals by holding a parade. In this case, the parade can celebrate the guest(s) of honor.

- Offer red and green fabric paints and inexpensive T-shirts to decorate and wear during the parade, and provide artificial cherries and glue from the craft store for ambitious designers.

- Give a prize for the most festive human "float" in the parade, or reward the guests who make up the best song about the guest(s) of honor.

Setting the Scene

- Play upbeat jazz or contemporary music, or music appropriate to the guest of honor. Some options are:

  Like Someone in Love by Ella Fitzgerald for a newly engaged couple or a couple celebrating an anniversary

  Workin' by Miles Davis for a promotion or new job

  Cherry Blossom by Keiko Matsui, a jazz album that continues the cherry theme

Zucchini Bites

To avoid overdoing the cherries in this meal, serve guests delicious veggies but keep a touch of red color. These baked zucchini treats are a great start to the meal.

Cooking spray
2 medium zucchini, cut into 3/4-inch rounds
1/2 cup reduced-fat baking mix
1/2 teaspoon garlic salt
1/2 teaspoon paprika
2 tablespoons grated Parmesan cheese

Preheat oven to 350°F. Heat cast-iron skillet or cookie sheet in oven for 2 minutes. Remove from oven.

Spray both sides of zucchini slices with cooking spray. Coat with baking mix.

Place zucchini slices in skillet or on cookie sheet and sprinkle with garlic salt, paprika, and Parmesan cheese.

Bake for 15 minutes until slightly browned.

Serve immediately.

Makes approximately 24 zucchini slices.
Serves 8.

purchasing tips for zucchini

When choosing zucchini, select those that are smaller in size. They will be more tender and have thinner skins. Buy only as many as you need; like most fruits and vegetables, zucchini tastes better when consumed shortly after purchase.

APPROXIMATE PER SERVING: *60 calories; 2.5 grams of fat*

Crispy Shrimp Sensations

Serve the shrimp alongside the zucchini for two crispy appetizers with very different flavors. The color of the cocktail sauce complements the other red dishes in this celebration.

1 pound medium shrimp, peeled and deveined (about 24 shrimp)
1/4 cup cornstarch
1 tablespoon water
2 large egg whites
1-1/2 cups finely crushed reduced-fat buttery crackers (about 35 crackers), such as Ritz
1 teaspoon paprika
1/4 teaspoon salt
1/4 teaspoon pepper
Cooking spray
1 12-ounce bottle cocktail sauce
Lemon wedges

Preheat broiler.

Place shrimp and cornstarch in a resealable plastic bag. Close bag and shake to coat.

In a small bowl, combine water and egg whites; beat until foamy.

In another small bowl, combine cracker crumbs, paprika, salt, and pepper.

Dip shrimp in egg white mixture, then coat with crumb mixture. Place on a baking sheet coated with cooking spray. Spray shrimp with a light coat of cooking spray.

Broil 5 minutes or until shrimp are done, turning once.

Serve with cocktail sauce and lemon wedges.

Serves 8.

preparation tips for shrimp

When you bring home fresh, uncooked shrimp, rinse them well under cold, running water and drain thoroughly. Tightly cover and refrigerate for up to 2 days or freeze for up to 3 months. Cooked shrimp can be refrigerated for up to 3 days. • Deveining is a matter of personal preference. For larger shrimp, however, the intestinal vein can contain grit, and it should be removed. (It's easier to peel and devein raw shrimp than cooked shrimp.)

APPROXIMATE PER SERVING: *310 calories; 4.5 grams of fat*

Cherry Limeade

This festive drink will refresh your guests.

3 liters lemon-lime soda
Ice cubes
3 cups cherry juice
2 limes, cut into fourths

Pour 1-1/2 cups of soda into each of 8 tall glasses filled with ice.
Add 1/3 cup of cherry juice to each glass.
Garnish each glass with a lime wedge.

Makes approximately 16 cups.
Serves 8.

cherry factoid

Cherries have been cultivated since 300 B.C., and they grew wild for many years prior.

APPROXIMATE PER SERVING: *110 calories; 2 grams of fat*

Roast Turkey Breast with Sour Cherry Sauce

It may be easiest to ask your butcher to cut two turkey breasts into 8 4-ounce pieces.

Turkey:
8 4-ounce turkey breast cutlets
2 medium onions, diced finely
2 teaspoons thyme
2 tablespoons poultry seasoning
1/2 teaspoon salt
Cooking Spray

Sauce:
1 cup cranberry juice cocktail
2 cups double-strength chicken stock
1 cup red tart cherries, fresh or frozen if available or canned, drained well
1 cup red tart cherries, puréed
1/8 teaspoon pepper
1/2 teaspoon bitters
2 tablespoons sugar
2 tablespoons plus 2 teaspoons cornstarch

Preheat oven to 350°F.

TO PREPARE TURKEY: Place turkey and onions in a small baking dish lightly coated with cooking spray.

Sprinkle with thyme, poultry seasoning, and salt. Cover with foil and cook 10 to 15 minutes until just done. Do not overcook.

TO PREPARE SAUCE: Bring cranberry juice, chicken stock, cherries, pepper, bitters, and sugar to a boil in a small saucepan.

Mix cornstarch in a small amount of water. Add to sauce and boil, stirring constantly, until thickened.

Remove from heat and serve over turkey.

Serves 8.

what are bitters?

Bitters, produced from the distillation of aromatic herbs, barks, roots, and plants, are a high-alcohol liquid used to flavor cocktails or foods.

APPROXIMATE PER SERVING: *260 calories; 9 grams of fat*

Crunchy Green Beans with Caramelized Onions

The red onion and imitation bacon bits offer a hint of cherry-red color in this delicious vegetable side dish.

1 large red onion, cut into 1/2-inch strips
1/2 teaspoon olive oil
2 pounds fresh green beans, washed and trimmed
1/2 teaspoon garlic salt
4 teaspoons balsamic vinegar
2 tablespoons imitation (soy) bacon bits

Heat olive oil in medium skillet. Add onion and sauté until golden brown (caramelized), stirring frequently, about 25 minutes. Set aside.

Steam green beans in steamer until crisp-tender, approximately 10 minutes.

Add green beans and garlic salt to skillet and mix with onions.

Drizzle with vinegar and sprinkle with bacon bits.

Serve warm or cold.

Serves 8.

no more tears with onions

To avoid teary eyes, peel onions under cold water. The water rinses away the volatile sulfur that causes teary eyes. You may also freeze the onion for 20 minutes before chopping.

APPROXIMATE PER SERVING: *80 calories; 2.5 grams of fat*

Brown Rice Pilaf

Brown rice takes longer to cook (approximately 40 minutes) than regular long-grain white rice (approximately 20 minutes). Quick brown rice cooks in 15 minutes and instant cooks in 10 minutes.

1 cup uncooked brown rice
2/3 cup onion, chopped
2/3 cup fresh mushrooms, sliced
1/8 teaspoon pepper (or to taste)
1/2 teaspoon fresh thyme or 1/4 teaspoon dried thyme
2-1/2 cups chicken broth
1 cup celery, thinly sliced

Preheat oven to 350°F.

Combine rice, onion, mushrooms, pepper, and thyme in a 1-quart casserole dish. Stir in broth. Cover and bake for 1 hour.

Add celery and mix well. Cover and bake for 10 to 15 minutes or until celery is just tender and liquid is absorbed.

Serves 8.

the life of brown rice

Brown rice is a nutritious member of the rice family. Because of its outer bran layer, it is higher in fiber, essential oils, most of the B vitamins, and minerals than white rice. Be sure to date your brown rice when you purchase it from the store. Brown rice has a shelf life of only 6 months.

APPROXIMATE PER SERVING: *107 calories; 1 gram of fat*

Cheery Cherry Parfaits

The acidic lemon juice prevents the cherries in this dish from becoming tinged with blue.

2 tablespoons cornstarch
1/2 teaspoon lemon juice
3 cups pitted dark sweet cherries (fresh, frozen, or canned), drained
3 cups pitted Royal Anne white cherries (fresh, frozen, or canned), drained
2 tablespoons light corn syrup
2 tablespoons sugar
1 cup low-fat cream cheese
4 cups plus 1/2 cup fat-free whipped topping, divided
Mint sprigs

Dissolve cornstarch in lemon juice.

In a large saucepan, mix together cornstarch mixture, cherries, corn syrup, and sugar. Bring to boil and simmer until thickened, approximately 3 to 5 minutes, stirring constantly.

Remove from heat and cool completely.

Beat together cream cheese and 4 cups of whipped topping until combined.

In glass parfait glasses, layer cream cheese mixture with cherry mixture twice, ending with cherries on top.

Top with a dollop of whipped topping and garnish with mint sprigs.

Serves 8.

cherries (Store unwashed cherries in a plastic bag in the refrigerator, and don't wash until just before eating. Allow cherries to sit out for a few hours before eating—their flavor is much better at room temperature. Fresh cherries should be consumed within two to four days.

APPROXIMATE PER SERVING: *340 calories; 8 grams of fat*

Home on the Range Hoedown

You can throw this country-and-western party anytime. June's pretty weather is the perfect time to horse around outside—and who needs a better excuse for a party?

menu for 8

- Spicy Salsa Dip
- Cowboy Cornbread
- Root Beer Floats
- Ranch Beans
- Texas Dry-Rub Barbecue
- Tri-Colored Jalapeño Slaw
- Country Corn on the Cob
- Round 'Em Up Oatmeal Carrot Bars

Invitations

- Use stamps and ink to decorate card stock with cowboy boots, rope, or cows, or purchase commercially available invitations.

- Trim card stock with strips of red bandana material or wrap the invitation in a bandana before putting in envelope. Put a few pieces of hay in each envelope.

- Provide bandanas at the door.

- SAMPLE WORDING: Join us at the Smiths' "barn" for a country hoedown, with all the dancin', wranglin', and eatin' you can stand. Come hungry and wear your cowboy gear!

Decorations

- Set out large hay bales for guests to sit on. Small bales are available at craft stores and work well on a buffet table as tiers for serving dishes.

- Wrap large #10 empty tin cans with red or blue bandanas and fill with utensils on the buffet table. Use thin rope to tie each napkin.

- Hang inexpensive cowboy hats on walls, on the front door, or on the table as part of a centerpiece.

Activity

- Get everybody dancing in between platefuls of your delicious food. Hold a square dance or use a video or a knowledgeable guest to teach the Texas Two-Step and other country line dances. Or for a big shindig, consider hiring an instructor.

- Set up a "cattle" lasso in the backyard outfitted with a rope and a stuffed animal cow or even a chair—anything that can be lassoed. Guests can compete to lasso the cow, winning extra points for style.

- Set up a game of horseshoes with prizes for winners. Make sure you know the rules and scoring—innings, ringers, and all!

Setting the Scene

- Play country-and-western music suited to specific line dances:
  Line Dance Party by Rousseau
  Line Dance Greatest Hits by various artists

- Or play traditional or contemporary country music in the background as guests eat. Some possibilities include:
  Road to Ensenada by Lyle Lovett
  Shotgun Willie by Willie Nelson
  Guitar Town by Steve Earle
  The Essential Vince Gill by Vince Gill
  Now That I've Found You: A Collection by Alison Krauss

- Play a how-to-line-dance video or old western on the VCR throughout the party:
  Christy Lane's Complete Guide to Line Dancing
  Line Dance 2001
  Big Country Line Dance Party

Spicy Salsa Dip

Make this salsa ahead of time so the flavors have time to meld.

3/4 cup bottled salsa
1/2 cup fresh cilantro leaves
2 teaspoons extra-virgin olive oil
1/4 teaspoon salt
2 drops hot pepper sauce
1 15-ounce can black beans, drained
Low-fat tortilla chips

Process all ingredients except tortilla chips in a food processor until smooth. Cover and refrigerate about 8 hours. Serve chilled or at room temperature, accompanied by tortilla chips.

Makes1-1/2 cups.
Serves 8.

salsa simplicity

To make your own easy salsa for this dish, combine 1/2 cup of chopped tomatoes, 1/4 cup of chopped onion, 1/8 cup of orange juice, 1/2 tablespoon of chopped cilantro, 1/2 tablespoon of lime juice, and 1/2 teaspoon of chopped jalapeño.

APPROXIMATE PER SERVING: *38 calories; 1 gram of fat*

Cowboy Cornbread

Butter-flavored cooking spray
2 cups self-rising cornmeal mix
2 tablespoons sugar
1 tablespoon brown sugar
1-1/2 cups 1% milk
1 egg, beaten
1 tablespoon canola oil
Half of a red bell pepper, finely diced
1 15-ounce can corn, drained
8 ounces fat-free cream cheese

Preheat oven to 425°F.

Coat a cast-iron skillet or an 8 × 8-inch baking dish with cooking spray.

In a medium bowl mix cornmeal, sugars, milk, egg, and canola oil until well blended.

Stir in bell pepper, corn, and cream cheese.

Pour into skillet and bake for 25 minutes until golden brown.

Serves 8.

cream of the crop — corn

There are more than 3,500 different uses for corn products and more are being found each day. There are uses for every part of the corn plant, even the water in which kernels are processed.

APPROXIMATE PER SERVING: *230 calories; 4.5 grams of fat*

Root Beer Floats

Although this frothy drink is bound to remind you of your childhood, you'll love it just as much now.

6 12-ounce cans root beer

1 half-gallon carton fat-free vanilla frozen yogurt

Pour root beer into tall glasses.

Spoon 1/2 cup of frozen yogurt into the top of each glass.

Serve with tall spoons or long drinking straws.

Makes approximately 8 cups of root beer floats.
Serves 8.

does root beer float?

Thomas Kemper Sodas set the world record for the world's largest root beer float in 1996. The Guinness Book of World Records measured the float at a whopping 2,166.5 gallons. The float occupied a 4,000-ton carbonation tank in Seattle, Washington, and used 900 gallons of ice cream that was donated by a local dairy. • The first root beer, credited to Charles Hire, contained some alcohol. Originally, it was sold as a temperance drink for alcoholics. In fact, during Prohibition, root beer was coined as the "Great American Temperance Drink."

APPROXIMATE PER SERVING: *260 calories; 0 grams of fat*

Ranch Beans

1 medium onion, diced
1 green pepper, diced
1 teaspoon canola oil
1 15-ounce can pinto beans, drained
2 15-ounce cans pinto beans, undrained
2 4-1/2-ounce cans chopped green chiles, undrained
1/4 cup imitation (soy) bacon bits

Heat oil in a medium saucepan over medium-high heat. Add diced onion and pepper and sauté until tender.

Add beans, chiles, and bacon bits. Reduce heat and simmer 20 minutes. Serve warm.

Serves 8.

ranch beans

Pinto is Spanish for "painted." • Pinto beans are also called red Mexican beans.

APPROXIMATE PER SERVING: *190 calories; 3.5 grams of fat*

Texas Dry-Rub Barbecue

*A **dry rub** is a mixture of dried herbs and seasonings rubbed onto meat or poultry and used to flavor the dish during the cooking process.*

2 pounds boneless top round steak or roast

Dry rub:
2 teaspoons chili powder
2 tablespoons dried onions
2 tablespoons cilantro
1/2 teaspoon dry mustard
1 dash cayenne pepper (optional)
2 tablespoons oregano
1/2 teaspoon cinnamon
2 teaspoons cumin
1/2 teaspoon garlic salt
2 tablespoons brown sugar
2 teaspoons canola oil

Sauce:
1/2 teaspoon catsup
2 tablespoons brown sugar
1/4 cup white vinegar
2 tablespoons honey
4 dashes hot sauce (or to taste)

Preheat oven to 300°F.

Trim fat from meat.

In a shallow bowl or plate, mix together the dry-rub ingredients (chili powder through brown sugar). Press rub onto both sides and edges of meat.

Lightly coat a small baking dish or pan with oil. Place meat in pan and cover tightly with foil.

Bake for 30 minutes. Remove from oven and allow to cool slightly. Chop meat into bite-sized pieces and return to baking dish.

In a small saucepan over medium-high heat, bring sauce ingredients to a boil. Cook sauce 2 minutes, then add to meat and pan drippings.

Serves 8.

bbq (The vinegar in barbecue sauce helps tenderize the meat.

APPROXIMATE PER SERVING: *190 calories; 5 grams of fat*

Tri-Colored Jalapeño Slaw

In case you're tempted to add more hot sauce, remember that this slaw will get spicier as it sits. The flavors meld as the cabbage "wilts" in the dressing.

1/4 medium red cabbage, cut into 1/2-inch ribbons
1/4 medium green cabbage, cut into 1/2-inch ribbons
4 large carrots, peeled into ribbons with a vegetable peeler
1 tablespoon pickled jalapeños, diced very finely
1/2 cup light coleslaw dressing
1 tablespoon juice from pickled jalapeños

In a large bowl, toss together cabbage, carrots, and jalapeños.

In a small bowl, whisk together coleslaw dressing and jalapeño juice.

Add dressing to cabbage mixture and toss to coat.

Serves 8.

pick a pepper

In general, the smaller the pepper, the hotter and spicier it tastes. The hottest parts of a hot pepper are the seeds and veins. • The jalapeño is ranked the third mildest hot pepper, after the El Paso and the Anaheim; the habañero is the hottest pepper and is approximately 30 to 50 percent hotter than the jalapeño. • Jalapeños are named after Jalapa, the capital of Veracruz, Mexico. • A dried jalapeño is called a chipotle. • Remember to wash your hands thoroughly after handling hot peppers.

APPROXIMATE PER SERVING: *50 calories; 1.5 grams of fat*

Country Corn on the Cob

8 ears fresh corn
1/3 cup fresh dill, minced (or 2 tablespoons dried dillweed)
1/3 cup fresh thyme, minced (or 2 tablespoons dried thyme)
2 tablespoons water
2 tablespoons corn oil or safflower oil
2 cloves garlic, minced

Preheat oven to 450°F.

Remove husks and silk from corn just before cooking.

Combine dill, thyme, water, oil, and garlic in a small bowl and mix well.

Place corn ears on squares of aluminum foil, brush each ear with mixture and wrap foil tightly around each.

Bake for 25 minutes, turning several times.

Serves 8.

purchasing tips for fresh corn

Corn is harvested between May and September. It's best to purchase and cook the corn as soon as it's picked, but it can be refrigerated without any ill effects for one day. Look for bright green ears. Pull the snugly fitted husk and golden brown silk back and look for uniform and tightly arranged rows of fleshy kernels that extend to the tip of the ear.

APPROXIMATE PER SERVING: *119 calories; 4 grams of fat*

Round 'Em Up Oatmeal Carrot Bars

3/4 cup light brown sugar, packed
1/4 cup corn oil margarine, softened
1 egg
1-1/2 to 2 cups carrots, shredded
1 teaspoon vanilla extract
1 cup whole-wheat flour
1 teaspoon baking powder
1 teaspoon cinnamon
1/4 teaspoon salt (optional)
1/2 to 3/4 cup uncooked oats
1/2 cup raisins
2 tablespoons wheat germ

Preheat oven to 350°F. Lightly grease an 8 × 8 baking pan. Set aside.

Cream brown sugar, margarine, and egg in a large mixing bowl until light and fluffy. Add carrots and vanilla, mixing well.

In a separate bowl, combine whole-wheat flour, baking powder, cinnamon, and salt. Add dry ingredients to creamed mixture and stir well.

Gently stir in oats, raisins, and wheat germ. Spread batter in pan.

Bake for 30 minutes or until set in center.

Allow to cool. Cut into 16 squares.

Serves 8.

oatmeal

Oat consumption has been found to lower cholesterol in adults. • Never substitute instant oats for rolled (also called old-fashioned) or quick-cooking oats. Instant oats have been precooked and can result in soggy baked products. Quick and rolled oats are interchangeable in most recipes.

APPROXIMATE PER SERVING: *89 calories; 3 grams of fat*

NOTES

Backyard Beach Barbecue

Turn your backyard into a beach by setting up kiddie pools (some filled with water and some with sand), a beach umbrella, and sand toys for a fun summertime party for adults and kids. Set up sprinklers with colorful spinning attachments to cool off guests as well.

menu for 8

- Red, Yellow, and Green Dip with Parmesan Pita Triangles
- Seaside Punch
- Skewered Shrimp, Chicken, and Pineapple with Honey-Orange Dipping Sauce
- Red Bliss Potato Salad
- Summer Fruit Salad with Poppy Seed Dressing
- White Bean Salad
- Lemon-Watermelon Slush

Invitations

- Decorate blue card stock with sand by spreading glue and sprinkling sand on top to stick. Glue a paper drink umbrella on the "beach" and print or write party information on the card. You might also want to draw or cut out pictures of fish, umbrella, or sand toys.

- SAMPLE WORDING: Please join us at the Cortez "beach," 1170 Main Street for a beach barbecue celebrating summer! Don't forget to bring a bathing suit and towel for cooling off…kiddie pool, sprinklers, sand, and sunscreen provided.

Decorations

- Purchase clean sand in bags or in bulk for kids to play in. Consider using a large plastic liner for sand if you want to remove it after the party or fill kiddie pools with sand to limit mess.

- Provide sand toys and put beach umbrellas in the ground. Fill kiddie pools with water and set up fun sprinklers for kids to run through.

- Serve food in brand-new plastic pails and beach toys and serve drinks chilled in a large galvanized aluminum tub filled with ice.

- Use bright madras plaid napkins and a tablecloth or set out giant colorful beach towels as tablecloths.

Activities

- Encourage guests to play with the beach props you've set up. Have sand-castle-building contests and a beach volleyball tournament if space allows.

Setting the Scene

- Play surf rock music to put guests in the mood for beach fun:
  Good Vibrations: Thirty Years of the Beach Boys by the Beach Boys
  King of the Surf Guitar: The Best of Dick Dale by Dick Dale
  Pipeline by The Chantays
  Wipe Out! The Best of the Surfaris by the Surfaris
  Surf City: The Best of Jan & Dean by Jan and Dean

Red, Yellow, and Green Dip with Parmesan Pita Triangles

Dip:
8 Roma tomatoes, seeded and diced
2 large green tomatoes, seeded and diced
2 yellow peppers, seeded and diced
1/4 teaspoon salt
1 teaspoon olive oil
1 tablespoon fresh oregano, chopped
2 teaspoons grated Parmesan cheese

Pita triangles:
6 whole-wheat pita bread pockets, cut into triangles
Cooking spray
1 tablespoon grated Parmesan cheese

Preheat oven to 400°F.

TO PREPARE DIP: In a small bowl mix together all dip ingredients except for cheese.

Place dip in serving bowl, sprinkle with Parmesan cheese, and chill.

TO PREPARE PITA: Place pita triangles on cooking sheet, lightly coat with cooking spray, and sprinkle with remaining Parmesan cheese.

Bake 10 minutes until crispy and lightly browned.

Cool slightly and serve with dip.

Serves 8.

eat a pita

Also called pocket bread, pita is a Middle Eastern flat bread made with white or whole-wheat flour.

APPROXIMATE PER SERVING: *179 calories; 2.5 grams of fat*

Seaside Punch

Add an ice mold to the punch bowl or serve the punch over ice.

2 1-quart bottles chilled cranberry juice cocktail
1 14-ounce can chilled unsweetened pineapple juice
2 cups ginger ale, chilled
2 cups seltzer water, chilled
Fresh pineapple and/or maraschino cherries for garnish, if desired

Combine juices, ginger ale, and seltzer water in a large punch bowl. Add garnish to punch bowl or individual glasses.

Makes 16 cups.
Serves 8.

make your own ice block

Pour water into a Jell-O mold or a Bundt pan. Freeze until solid. To remove the ice mold, immerse into hot tap water for 3 minutes or until sides appear melted. Invert the mold onto wax paper, plastic wrap, or aluminum foil. Place in punch bowl before mixing punch.

APPROXIMATE PER SERVING: *190 calories; 0 grams of fat*

Skewered Shrimp, Chicken, and Pineapple
with Honey-Orange Dipping Sauce

For skewers:

12 large shrimp (31–40 count; about 6 ounces), cleaned, deveined, tails on

4 skinless, boneless chicken breasts, cut into 1-1/2-inch cubes

2 cups pineapple chunks

2 tablespoons pineapple juice

1/2 teaspoon garlic salt

Sauce:

2 teaspoons cornstarch

1/4 teaspoon lemon juice

1 cup orange juice

2 tablespoons honey

1 dash pepper

Wooden skewers, soaked in water

TO PREPARE SKEWERS: Thread shrimp, chicken, and pineapple on water-soaked wooden skewers, alternating shrimp and chicken with pineapple chunks. Place in shallow dish and sprinkle with pineapple juice.

Heat grill to medium, place skewers on grill surface, and sprinkle with garlic salt.

Cook 2 to 3 minutes per side until shrimp turn pink and chicken is completely cooked through. Remove from grill to a serving platter.

TO PREPARE SAUCE: Dissolve cornstarch in lemon juice.

In a small saucepan stir together orange juice, honey, and pepper. Bring to boil and stir in cornstarch mixture.

Cook 2 to 3 minutes until thickened. Remove from heat.

Serve skewers with dipping sauce.

Serves 8.

avoid a sticky situation

Before measuring sticky ingredients, such as honey or syrup, use cooking spray in your measuring cups or spoons. Not only will all of the sticky stuff pour easily, it's also easy to clean up.

APPROXIMATE PER SERVING: *200 calories; 2 grams of fat*

Red Bliss Potato Salad

8 medium red potatoes, skins on, scrubbed, cut into eighths
1 teaspoon salt
2/3 cup light mayonnaise
1 1-ounce package dry ranch salad dressing mix
4 stalks celery, chopped finely
1 red bell pepper, chopped finely
2 scallions, chopped finely

Place potatoes in a large saucepan, cover with water, add salt, and bring to boil. Boil 10 minutes until tender and drain well. Return potatoes to pan.

Mix mayonnaise and dressing mix in a small bowl. Stir into hot potatoes to coat.

Add celery, red pepper, and all but 2 tablespoons of scallions to potato mixture.

Transfer to serving dish and top with remaining scallions.

Serve warm or cold.

Serves 8.

tuber trivia

Peel or remove any green spots on potatoes before preparing them. These spots are the result of prolonged light exposure and cause the potato to taste bitter. To keep potatoes fresh for up to 2 months, place in a brown paper bag with an apple. The apple emits ethylene gas that prevents the potatoes from sprouting. Potatoes are not botanically related to sweet potatoes or yams.

APPROXIMATE PER SERVING: *210 calories; 9 grams of fat*

Summer Fruit Salad with Poppy Seed Dressing

For this salad we used equal parts peeled peaches and oranges, chunks of pineapple, grapes, and berries. Use any fruit you like.

8 cups fresh fruit, cut into bite-sized pieces

2-2/3 cups low-fat vanilla yogurt

1 teaspoon poppy seeds

Combine all fruit in a large bowl.

In a smaller bowl, fold poppy seeds into yogurt with a whisk or spatula.

Spoon a portion of fruit salad into individual serving dishes, then pour 2 to 3 tablespoons of yogurt mixture over the fruit—or set out the fruit salad and yogurt dressing separately and invite your guests to help themselves.

Makes 8 cups.
Serves 8.

yogurt is your friend

Yogurt is an excellent source of B vitamins, protein, and calcium. Some experts claim that yogurt, when ingested, inhabits the intestinal tract with good bacteria and maintains it in good working order.

APPROXIMATE PER SERVING: *184 calories; 1.5 grams of fat*

White Bean Salad

Serve this salad with simple crostini.

Salad Dressing:
2 teaspoons olive oil, divided
1 garlic clove, minced
1 teaspoon dried oregano
1/4 cup cider vinegar

Bean Salad:
2 16-ounce cans cannellini beans or other white beans, rinsed and drained
1-1/2 cups diced plum tomato
1/2 cup chopped Vidalia or other sweet onion
1/2 cup (2 ounces) crumbled blue cheese
1/3 cup chopped fresh parsley
1/2 teaspoon salt
1/2 teaspoon ground pepper

Crostini:
Two loaves deli-style bread (French, Italian, or whole-wheat, for example)

TO PREPARE SALAD DRESSING: In a nonstick skillet, heat 1 teaspoon of olive oil over medium-high heat. Add the garlic and oregano; sauté for 30 seconds. Remove from heat and stir in vinegar.

TO PREPARE THE SALAD: In a large bowl, combine remaining teaspoon of olive oil and the next 7 ingredients (beans through pepper).

Add the dressing to the bean salad; toss lightly.

Cover and chill for 30 minutes before serving.

TO PREPARE CROSTINI: Slice bread thinly. Toast under a broiler or in the toaster. Top with bean salad.

Serves 8.

the bean scene

Cannellini beans are large white Italian kidney beans. Great Northern beans, which look like white lima beans, can be substituted for cannellini beans in most recipes.

APPROXIMATE PER SERVING: *289 calories; 6 grams of fat*

Lemon-Watermelon Slush

1 cup lemon juice, freshly squeezed, with pulp (from approximately 4 large lemons)
1/2 cup sugar
8 cups seeded, diced watermelon
30 to 40 ice cubes
2 tablespoons fresh mint for garnish

In a small saucepan, bring lemon juice and sugar to a boil. Stir until all sugar is dissolved and remove from heat. Chill syrup well.

Blend in four batches. For each batch, place 2 cups of watermelon into blender, add 1/4 of the chilled lemon syrup, and blend until mixed well.

Add ice cubes to blender one at a time, approximately 10 per batch, until mixture is thickened.

Repeat for remaining three batches.

Serve in chilled glasses and garnish with fresh mint.

Serves 8.

how to choose a watermelon

Because watermelon do not ripen off the vine, it is important to choose those that are ripe. There are two methods: appearance and sound. On first inspection, choose a symmetrical melon that is heavy for its size and has a dull green, firm rind. Turn the melon on its underside–it should be yellow. Next, perform the slap test. Using a flattened palm, smack the melon. A hollow or deep-pitched tone indicates ripeness. A high-pitched tone is a sign of an under-ripe melon and dull thud indicates over-ripeness.

APPROXIMATE PER SERVING: *100 calories; 0.5 grams of fat*

NOTES

NOTES

Jamaican Jam

This outside party with a tropical twist features classic island dishes like Jerk shrimp and plantains. It's fun to hold this party in the heat of summer, but true to Jamaican style, anything goes—including having this party in the dead of winter, if you want to spice things up. Get friends together anytime for delicious Caribbean food and fun.

menu for 8

- Jerk Shrimp with Berry Sauce
- Montego Bay Papaya Punch
- Coconut-Rum Salmon
- Black Beans and Rice with Papaya and Red Onions
- Baked Sweet Potato Wedges
- Tropical Fruit Display
- Banana Custard

Invitations

- Make your own tropical invitations by gluing silk hibiscus flowers to brightly colored card stock and writing party information on the card. Or use large silk banana leaves as a background and glue card stock with party information onto them. Fold the leaves over the card stock to fit the invitations into envelopes. Or simply look for brightly colored or flowered invitations and fill in your party information.

- You can even use concentrated coconut or pineapple oil to scent the invitations. (But be sure not to smear the party invitation with the oil, which is available in the potpourri-making section of craft stores or in specialty shops.)

Decorations

- Use tropical colors, such as hot pink, salmon, bright yellow, bright green, and turquoise, to decorate. Add varied colors of solid napkins to a floral tablecloth. Use potted hibiscus plants on the table and in the entryway.

- Arrange coconuts, bananas, mangoes, pineapples, and/or papayas in a large basket as a centerpiece. Serve food on glass or brightly colored platters surrounded by silk banana leaves.

- If you want, offer pieces of sugarcane for guests to try. Sugarcane is available at some farmers' markets and specialty grocery stores.

Activity

- Clear a space and hold a limbo contest. Don't forget you'll need a pole or rod for people to scoot under and limbo music!

Setting the Scene

- Play some reggae to get people in the Jamaican state of mind:
  Very Best of Toots & the Maytals by Toots & the Maytals
  Nyah Man Chant by Bushman
  Equal Rights by Peter Tosh
  Legend by Bob Marley
  Party dance music including *Limbo*

Jerk Shrimp with Berry Sauce

You may substitute prepared mustard for dry mustard in most recipes. For every teaspoon of dry mustard, use a tablespoon of prepared mustard.

24 large shrimp (about 12 ounces, or 31-40 count) cleaned, deveined, tails on

Marinade:
1/4 cup fat-free raspberry vinaigrette
2 teaspoons allspice
1/2 teaspoon dry mustard
Dash of cayenne pepper
1/4 teaspoon garlic salt

Sauce:
1/4 cup raspberry fruit spread
1/4 cup blueberry fruit spread
2 tablespoons light corn syrup

Place shrimp in a small bowl.

TO PREPARE THE MARINADE: Mix together vinaigrette, allspice, mustard, cayenne, and garlic salt. Pour over shrimp. Marinate for 1 hour.

Heat grill to medium heat. Place shrimp directly on heated grill surface. Grill for 1 to 2 minutes per side until firm and pink. Do not overcook.

TO PREPARE SAUCE: Heat fruit spreads and corn syrup in small saucepan until boiling.

Remove from heat and serve with hot shrimp.

Serves 8.

make your own jerk seasoning

Combine chiles of your choosing (crushed red pepper, cayenne, dried jalapeno, and/or other chile pepper), thyme, cinnamon, ginger, allspice, cloves, powdered garlic, and dried onion. Experiment with amounts of each ingredient to achieve the flavor you desire. Use your mixture as a rub, or mix the seasonings with teriyaki or other liquid to create a marinade.

APPROXIMATE PER SERVING: *96 calories; 1 gram of fat*

Montego Bay Papaya Punch

4 cups ice cubes
2 small ripe papayas, peeled and cut into chunks
2 cups guava nectar
4 tablespoons sugar
Pinch of salt
1-1/3 cups milk

Blend in batches.

For each batch, put ice in blender and blend on high until crushed. Add half of a papaya, 1/2 cup of guava nectar, 1 tablespoon of sugar, and pinch of salt. Blend until slushy. Add 1/3 cup of milk and blend again. Serve immediately.

Blend remaining batches, serving each immediately.

Serves 8.

papaya's good for ya

Papaya is an excellent source of vitamin C, which is essential for healthy skin and connective tissues, for normal chemical and hormonal production, and aids the immune system. Half of a medium-sized papaya supplies 150% of your recommended daily allowance of vitamin C.

APPROXIMATE PER SERVING: *84 calories; 1 gram of fat*

Coconut-Rum Salmon

3 cups light or dark rum
1/4 cup brown sugar
1/4 cup molasses
8 4-ounce boneless salmon steaks, about 1-inch thick
1/4 cup flaked sweetened coconut
1 teaspoon garlic salt
1 teaspoon paprika

Preheat oven to 400°F.

In a medium saucepan, bring rum and brown sugar to a boil; lower heat to medium-high and cook 3 minutes.

Cool rum mixture and stir in molasses.

Place salmon steaks on nonstick baking pan. Baste both sides with rum sauce.

Press coconut onto top of steaks; sprinkle with garlic salt and paprika.

Bake approximately 10 minutes or until center is cooked through, basting halfway through cooking.

Place steaks on a heated serving dish and pour remaining sauce over top.

Serves 8.

there's nothing fishy about salmon

Salmon is a very nutritious food; it is high in vitamin A, B-complex, and omega-3 oils. Research is exploring omega-3 fatty acids' potential suppression of cancer formation.

APPROXIMATE PER SERVING: *420 calories; 8 grams of fat*

Black Beans and Rice with Papaya and Red Onions

The small, shiny, grayish seeds of the papaya can be eaten. They are mild and peppery in taste. Try them on top of this dish or in a salad.

1 red onion, chopped finely, divided in half
1 teaspoon olive oil
1 15-ounce can black beans, drained
1 15-ounce can black beans, undrained
1/2 teaspoon ginger
1/4 teaspoon allspice
1/4 teaspoon garlic salt
2 cups fat-free chicken broth
1 cup brown rice
1 small papaya, peeled, seeded, and diced
2 scallions, chopped

Heat oil in a medium saucepan over medium-high heat, and sauté half of the onion until tender. Add beans, ginger, allspice, and garlic salt and bring to a boil.

Reduce heat and simmer 20 minutes, mashing half of the beans with a fork after 10 minutes to thicken.

In another medium saucepan, bring chicken broth to boil and add rice. Reduce heat and simmer 45 minutes.

Transfer rice to serving dish; spoon beans over rice.

Top with papaya, red onion, and scallions.

Serves 8.

particulars of purchasing papayas

When picking papayas at the store, choose vivid gold-yellow fruit with a shiny texture. The flesh should give slightly to gentle pressure. Greenish papayas, if left out at room temperature, will ripen quickly. To accelerate ripening, place fruit in a paper bag. To ripen papayas even faster, add a banana to the bag. Use ripe papayas immediately or refrigerate up to 3 days. Once refrigerated, the ripening process stops permanently.

APPROXIMATE PER SERVING: *420 calories; 8 grams of fat*

Baked Sweet Potato Wedges

Cooking spray
4 large sweet potatoes, scrubbed, eyes removed, cut lengthwise into 3/4-inch wedges
1 teaspoon paprika
1 tablespoon brown sugar
1 teaspoon garlic salt
1 teaspoon cinnamon
Dash of cayenne pepper (optional)

Preheat oven to 400°F.

Lightly spray nonstick baking dish or cast-iron skillet with cooking spray.

Spray potato wedges with cooking spray and toss together with all spices in a bowl.

Place potatoes in a single layer in the baking dish or skillet. Bake for 20 minutes. Turn over and bake an additional 20 minutes.

Serves 8.

sweet potatoes or yams?

Sweet potatoes pack a powerful vitamin A punch—one medium sweet potato provides 520% of your recommended daily allowance! • Americans sometimes call dark-skinned sweet potatoes "yams," which are actually a different plant species from the sweet potato. Neither the dark-skinned nor the light-skinned sweet potatoes widely available in the United States are yams. Yams, which may have skin ranging in color from off-white to dark brown and flesh from off-white and yellow to purple ad pink, are popular in South and Central America, the West Indies, and parts of Asia and Africa.

APPROXIMATE PER SERVING: *125 calories; 0 grams of fat*

Tropical Fruit Display

Offer a selection of the following: kiwi, pineapple, mango, papaya, and banana.

Peel and slice kiwi, pineapple, mango, papaya, and banana. Reserve large slices of fruit for garnish and cut the rest into bite-sized pieces. Sprinkle banana with lemon juice to avoid browning. Arrange fruit and garnish on a platter in a rainbow of color.

what's in a name?

Kiwifruit is also known as the Chinese gooseberry because of the fruit's place of origin. The name kiwifruit is thought to have been inspired by New Zealand's national bird, the kiwi, whose fuzzy brown exterior resembles that of the fruit. • The English coined the name pineapple. The Spanish name for pinecone is pina, and the fruit does resemble a pinecone. The name stuck for Latin Americans, who refer to the pineapple as pina. • The English name banana evolved from its Guinean name banema.

Calories and fat will vary depending on ingredients and serving size.

Banana Custard

This simple and delicious recipe is an easy dessert. Serve with cookies of your choice.

3 to 4 cups ripe banana
2 tablespoons lime or lemon juice
1/4 cup evaporated skim milk
1-1/2 cups yogurt (plain, vanilla, or banana)

Place bananas in a blender and mash with a spatula or spoon. Add evaporated milk and lime or lemon juice. Blend for 30 seconds.

Add yogurt and blend for another 30 seconds.

Spoon 1/4 cup of mixture into each dessert bowl. Chill for 2 to 3 hours.

Serve with your favorite cookies.

Serves 8.

ripen bananas quickly

To ripen green bananas quickly, place them in a perforated brown paper bag and store in a warm, dry place, such as on top of the refrigerator. Bananas also ripen fruit that is in their vicinity, so if you don't want that peach or pear to ripen further, separate them from your bananas.

APPROXIMATE PER SERVING: *102 calories; 1 gram of fat*

NOTES

NOTES

Salsa Party

Throw a spirited summer party featuring salsa and mambo music and dancing. Ask guests to bring their favorite salsa recipes to spice up the menu, and assemble an array of flavors for a salsa tasting and competition.

menu for 8

- Corn, Onion, Red Pepper, White Bean, and Cilantro Salsa
- Pineapple, Peach, and Jalapeño Salsa
- Sangría Blanca Punch
- Mexican Chicken Salad
- Black Bean–Filled Sweet Potato Biscuits with Queso Fresco
- Jicama Slaw
- Caribbean Rice and Beans
- Key Lime Yogurt Pie

Invitations

- Send out brightly colored invitations, handmade or purchased. A maraca design is always fun.
- SAMPLE WORDING: Come to a Spicy Summer Salsa Party • Saturday night • Casual dinner and dancing • Please bring your favorite salsa and copies of the recipe.

Decorations

- Use a red, green, and yellow color scheme for the tablecloth and napkins.
- Arrange bright flowers in vases filled with dried black beans (use the beans to keep the flowers arranged) and water.
- Set out a few sets of maracas on the table (available at craft stores) and serve food in rustic pottery serving pieces if you have them.

Activities

- SALSA AND MAMBO DANCING: Consider hiring an instructor or asking a knowledgeable friend to lead dancing. For a simpler approach, use one of the suggested dance videos below. Encourage everyone to get into the action.

- SALSA TASTING: Ask guests to taste and vote for the best salsa. Give out prizes of salsa music CDs for categories like hottest, most colorful, most unusual, and so on. Offer recipes for people to take home.

Setting the Scene

- Play mambo and salsa music to keep everyone moving, such as:
  The Mambo King by Tito Puente
  Uno, Dos, Tres by Willie Bobo
  When the Night Is Over by Little Louie and Marc Anthony

- Use a how-to videotape to teach your guests how to dance Latin-style. Possibilities include:
  Latin Dancing for Beginners
  Cal Pozo's Learn to Dance in Minutes—The Latin Dances (or Salsa)
  You Can Dance: Mambo
  You Can Dance: Cha-Cha
  You Can Dance: Rhumba
  You Can Dance: Lambada
  Red Hot Salsa—Learn to Salsa With Ron & Bethana Rosario

Corn, Onion, Red Pepper, White Bean, and Cilantro Salsa

Chopped tomatoes, vegetables, and salsa spices are virtually fat free. Serve this loaded salsa with tortilla chips.

1 15-ounce can Great Northern white beans, rinsed and drained well
1 15-ounce can yellow corn, drained well
1 large red bell pepper, diced finely
1 large yellow onion, diced finely
1/2 cup fresh cilantro, chopped finely
1 tablespoon lime juice
1 tablespoon jalapeño (green) hot pepper sauce
Dash of salt
1/2 lime, sliced thinly for garnish
1 tablespoon cilantro leaves for garnish

In a large bowl, mix together beans, corn, red pepper, onion, and cilantro.

In a small bowl, mix together lime juice, hot pepper sauce, and salt.

Toss lime juice mixture with bean mixture.

Transfer to serving bowl.

Garnish with additional lime slices and cilantro, if desired.

Serves 8.

time-saving tip

Many dishes in this theme contain onions and cilantro. Save yourself time—and in the case of the onions, tears—by chopping more than you need for one recipe. Store extra chopped onions in a resealable bag or container for up to 5 days and extra chopped cilantro for up to 2 days. Chopped cilantro (as well as parsley) can also be frozen for 2 months and then used in cooked or baked dishes.

APPROXIMATE PER SERVING: *130 calories; 1 gram of fat*

Pineapple, Peach, and Jalapeño Salsa

Before you add more jalapeños, remember that the salsa will get hotter as it sits. Serve this sweet-hot salsa with salty tortilla chips.

2 cups pineapple, chopped finely
2 cups peaches, chopped finely
4 pickled jalapeño slices, minced
2 scallions, chopped finely, divided
1/4 teaspoon garlic salt

In a medium bowl, mix all ingredients together except for 1 tablespoon of scallions.

Transfer to serving bowl, top with remaining scallions, and chill 1 hour.

Serves 8.

symbolic fruits

The pineapple is a widely recognized symbol of hospitality, and in ancient Chinese culture, the peach was a symbol of immortality.

APPROXIMATE PER SERVING: *48 calories; 0 grams of fat*

Sangría Blanca Punch

This nonalcoholic drink will cool off your guests during the salsa tasting. For an authentic touch, add fruit such as fresh pineapple, frozen grapes, maraschino cherries, or orange slices.

4-1/2 cups pineapple juice
1-1/2 cups white grape juice
1-1/2 cups passion fruit juice
1/2 cup fresh lime juice
2 12-ounce cans ginger ale

Combine all juices in a punch bowl. Chill.

Just before serving, add ginger ale, stirring gently. Serve in cups with ice.

Serves 8.

what is sangria?

Derived from *Sangre,* the Spanish word for blood, sangría is traditionally made with red wine, fruit juices, soda water, fruit, and sometimes brandy or cognac. Sangría blanca is made with white wine.

APPROXIMATE PER SERVING: *90 calories; 0 grams of fat*

Mexican Chicken Salad

1 medium head lettuce, shredded
1 15-ounce can black beans, drained
1 cup cooked skinless chicken, chopped
1/2 cup green bell pepper, seeded and chopped
2 scallions, chopped
1/2 cup fresh cilantro, chopped
3 tablespoons chicken broth
2 tablespoons corn oil or safflower oil
2 tablespoons red wine vinegar
1 tablespoon fresh lime juice
1-1/2 teaspoons granulated sugar
1 clove of garlic, minced
3/4 teaspoon chili powder
1/2 teaspoon salt (optional)

Place lettuce, beans, chicken, green pepper, and scallions in a salad bowl.

Combine cilantro, broth, oil, vinegar, lime juice, sugar, garlic, chili powder, and salt in a blender and process until well mixed.

Pour over chicken salad just before serving and toss lightly.

Serves 8.

handling raw meat

Remember to use safe handling practices when cooking with raw chicken or meat. This includes: thawing frozen meat in the refrigerator or microwave, washing your hands before and after handling raw meat, washing utensils and cutting boards in hot soapy water, cooking raw chicken thoroughly, and preventing raw meat and juices from coming in contact with other foods. Following these safety tips should reduce your risk of contracting a food-borne illness.

APPROXIMATE PER SERVING: *164 calories; 5 grams of fat*

Black Bean–Filled Sweet Potato Biscuits with Queso Fresco

Queso fresco, also called queso blanco, is a white, fresh Mexican cheese. It's available in Latin markets and many supermarkets. If you can't find it, use jack cheese instead.

Biscuits:
2-1/2 cups reduced-fat baking mix
3/4 cup 1% milk
1 cup sweet potato, peeled, cooked, mashed well

Beans:
1 teaspoon olive oil
1 small onion, diced finely
1 large carrot, sliced into thin coins
1 teaspoon cumin
1 teaspoon chili powder
1 teaspoon cilantro, fresh or dried
1 teaspoon green jalapeño (hot pepper) sauce, such as Tabasco®
1 15-ounce can black beans, drained
1 15-ounce can black beans, undrained

1/2 cup fresh cilantro, chopped
1/2 cup queso fresco, shredded (or crumbled jack cheese)

TO PREPARE BISCUITS: Preheat oven to 450°F.

Mix together baking mix and milk to form dough. Mix in sweet potato. Turn dough onto surface sprinkled with baking mix. Knead 10 times and roll out to 1/2-inch thick.

Using a 3-inch round biscuit cutter, cut dough into 8 biscuits. Place on ungreased cookie sheet and bake until golden brown, about 8 minutes.

Remove from oven and cool.

Form a cup in each biscuit by cutting out a circle on the top and scooping out some of the insides. Reserve the cut-out tops.

TO PREPARE BEANS: Heat olive oil in a medium-sized saucepan over medium-high heat. Sauté onion until tender. Add carrots, spices, hot pepper sauce, and beans. Bring to a boil.

Reduce heat and simmer 10 minutes. Mash half of bean mixture with a fork. This will cause the mixture to thicken. Simmer an additional 10 minutes, stirring occasionally.

To serve, fill each biscuit with bean mixture until slightly overflowing.

Top with queso fresco and fresh cilantro. Place one reserved cut-out top on top of each biscuit partially revealing the filling.

Serves 8.

tabasco facts

Edmund McIlhenny created Tabasco in 1868 on Avery Island, Louisiana, where the company is still in operation today. He received a patent for his hot sauce in 1870.

APPROXIMATE PER SERVING: *308 calories; 6 grams of fat*

Jícama Slaw

1 large jicama, peeled and cut into fine strips
2 tablespoons lemon juice, divided
1 sweet red pepper, cut into fine strips
1 cup purple cabbage, cut into fine strips
1 tablespoon honey

Toss jicama with 1 tablespoon of lemon juice immediately upon cutting to prevent browning.

Mix jicama, red pepper, and cabbage in medium bowl.

Whisk remaining 1 tablespoon of lemon juice together with honey and toss with slaw to coat.

Chill and toss again before serving to distribute dressing.

Serves 8.

hik'-e ma—huh?

Jicama is a large root vegetable. It has a thin brown skin that should be peeled before eating and a white, crunchy interior. Delicious either raw or cooked, jicama has a sweet, nutty flavor with a crisp texture. Store your jicamas in a plastic bag in the refrigerator for up to 2 weeks.

APPROXIMATE PER SERVING: *88 calories; 0 grams of fat*

Caribbean Rice and Beans

1-1/3 cups water
1-1/3 cups uncooked instant rice
2 teaspoons vegetable oil
2 cups chopped onion
1 cup chopped celery
1 cup green bell pepper, cored, seeded, and diced
6 garlic cloves, minced
2 15-ounce cans black beans, drained
2 cups coarsely chopped tomatoes
1/4 teaspoon salt
1/2 teaspoon crushed red pepper
1/2 teaspoon ground cumin
1/2 cup chopped fresh cilantro
1 cup part-skim mozzarella cheese, shredded

Cook rice according to package directions.

Heat oil on medium-high in a large nonstick pan. Add onion, celery, bell pepper, garlic, and black beans. Sauté until tender, about 5 minutes.

Add tomatoes, salt, crushed red pepper, and cumin to the pan. Sauté for 2 minutes.

Stir in cooked rice and cilantro. Cook until thoroughly heated.

Place on serving dish and sprinkle with cheese.

Makes approximately 8 cups.
Serves 8.

more cilantro

Cilantro will stay fresh for up to one week in the refrigerator if loosely wrapped in a moist paper towel and placed in a plastic baggie. Another way to keep cilantro fresh is to place the bunch, stems down, in a glass of water and cover with a plastic bag. Seal the bag with a rubber band and refrigerate. Change the water every 2 to 3 days.

APPROXIMATE PER SERVING: *256 calories; 6 grams of fat*

Key Lime Yogurt Pie

1-1/4 cups graham cracker crumbs
2 tablespoons margarine, melted
1/2 cup frozen apple juice concentrate, thawed
1 envelope unflavored gelatin
2 tablespoons sugar
1/3 cup fresh lime juice
2 teaspoons lime zest
1/4 teaspoon vanilla extract
1-1/2 cups low-fat plain yogurt
Fresh lime slices for garnish

Combine crumbs and margarine in a small bowl and mix well. Press crumb mixture over bottom and side of a pie plate and freeze.

Pour apple juice into a saucepan, sprinkle with gelatin, and let stand for several minutes or until gelatin is softened.

Add sugar and cook over low heat until gelatin and sugar dissolve, stirring constantly.

Pour gelatin mixture into a mixer bowl. Add lime juice, zest, and vanilla.

Chill until mixture resembles raw egg whites, then beat until fluffy. Add yogurt, continuing to beat until fluffy.

Pour yogurt mixture into prepared crust and chill until firm.
Garnish with lime slices.

Serves 8.

fine limes

British sailors stocked their boats with limes to ward off scurvy, a debilitating disease caused by a vitamin C deficiency. Hence British seamen were nicknamed "limeys." • Key limes are more yellow than green. So beware if you see a green key lime pie! • When choosing a lime, look for bright green fruit that feels heavy for its size. Small brown marks on the skin will not affect the flavor of the lime. Refrigerate limes in a plastic bag for up to 10 days.

APPROXIMATE PER SERVING: *152 calories; 5 grams of fat*

NOTES

NOTES

Croquet Classic

This elegant summer party can include a backyard croquet competition. This menu is appropriate for a pre-wedding party, anniversary, shower, or just for celebrating a summer afternoon.

menu for 8

- Dilled Salmon Mousse
- Mini Bean Croquettes with Tomato-Anchovy Dip
- Summer Sparkler
- Julienned Carrot and Celery Orzo
- Seared Sesame Scallops with Avocado Sauce
- Zucchini and Squash Tart
- Summer Strawberry Shortcake

Invitations

- Make a croquet wicket by bending silver craft wire into an arch, then glue it to card stock. Paint "grass" with a paintbrush and green paint and cut a croquet ball out of colored card stock to paste on—don't forget to paint or draw the stripes on the ball.

- SAMPLE WORDING: Please join the Smiths for a croquet party and luncheon to celebrate summer. Wear white and pastels in the style of dapper dressers of the past—boater hats, bow ties, and all-white attire are all appropriate.

Decorations

- Cover the buffet table with white or pastel linen tablecloths and napkins. Pair a variety of napkins in different pastel colors with a white tablecloth, for example.

- Keep the theme light and bright by serving the meal in all-white or clear glass serving pieces. Line baskets with pastel linen napkins and fill with crackers. Offer a variety of pastel plates or all-white plates.

- Arrange a mix of elegant pastel flowers in a large white pitcher or large glass vase filled with whole lemons, limes, and water.

Activities

- Hold a croquet competition and have winners play each other until one winner remains. Don't forget to set up the croquet set and brush up on the rules. The United States Croquet Association or World of Croquet web sites can help you find equipment and learn about croquet.

- Offer prizes to the tournament winner, but reward other "achievements" as well, such as best croquet outfit and most sportsmanlike play. Gifts that hearken back to the 1920s could include: Picasso postcards, a mah-jongg game, music from the era, or a book about Charles Lindbergh, such as *An American Hero* by Barry Denenberg.

- You can also hold an old-fashioned hoop race using hula hoops or hold a Charleston competition.

Setting the Scene

- Play some 1920s-style music to take your guests back to the early days of jazz:
  New Orleans Rhythm Kings and Jelly Roll Morton by the New Orleans Rhythm Kings
  Djangologie by Django Reinhardt
  Bix Beiderbecke, Vol. 1 or *Bix Beiderbecke, Vol. 2* by Bix Beiderbecke
  Flaming Youth by Duke Ellington
  Indispensable by Fletcher Henderson

- Set up a video of *The Great Gatsby* for guests who wish to relax indoors.

Dilled Salmon Mousse

You'll need a mold for this retro party food. Before serving, arrange crackers or chopped fresh vegetables around the mousse.

1/4 cup water or clam juice
1/2 envelope unflavored gelatin
1/4 cup low-fat cottage cheese
1/2 to 1 tablespoon 1% milk
6 tablespoons low-fat plain yogurt
1/4 cup celery, finely chopped
1 tablespoon fresh dill, minced, or 1/2 tablespoon dried dillweed
1-1/2 teaspoon onion, grated
1-1/2 teaspoon fresh lemon juice
1/2 teaspoon salt (optional)
Dash of hot sauce
1 7-1/2-ounce can sockeye salmon, drained

Place cold water or clam juice in a small saucepan. Sprinkle gelatin over liquid and let stand for 5 minutes. Dissolve gelatin over medium heat. Cool to room temperature.

In a blender, mix cottage cheese and enough milk to combine ingredients. Process until smooth.

Stir cottage cheese mixture, yogurt, celery, dill, onion, lemon juice, salt, and hot sauce into the gelatin mixture.

In a bowl, mash salmon with a fork or blend in a food processor until finely flaked.

Fold salmon into cheese mixture and spoon into a 4-cup mold. Cover and chill for 3 hours or until firm.

Unmold mousse onto a serving dish.

Serves 8.

unmolding made easy

Coat the mold with vegetable cooking spray before filling it. When congealed, gently ease the mixture away from the edge of the mold with your fingers. Invert the mold over the serving platter and gently shake it up and down until the gelled mixture drops out. If the mold won't release, leave it upside-down on the dish and cover with a warm, damp towel for a few seconds, then shake the mold again.

APPROXIMATE PER SERVING: *54 calories; 2 grams of fat*

Mini Bean Croquettes with Tomato-Anchovy Dip

Anchovy paste is a nice alternative to canned anchovies and allows you to control the amount of flavor and saltiness you want.

Croquettes:
1 cup cooked chickpeas, drained well, mashed with fork
2 tablespoons parsley, chopped finely
1/8 teaspoon black pepper
1/4 teaspoon garlic salt
1/2 teaspoon lemon juice
1/8 teaspoon hot sauce
2 eggs, beaten
2/3 cup seasoned breadcrumbs
Cooking spray

Sauce:
2 cups tomato sauce
1 teaspoon olive oil
2 teaspoons anchovy paste
4 tablespoons seasoned breadcrumbs

TO PREPARE CROQUETTES: In a large bowl, mix together chickpeas, parsley, pepper, garlic salt, lemon juice, and hot sauce. Mix in eggs.

Stir in breadcrumbs and form mixture into tablespoon-sized balls.

Heat a large nonstick or cast-iron skillet on medium-high and coat with cooking spray.

Drop croquettes onto hot skillet and cook 1 minute on all sides until browned and crispy.

(continued on next page)

Remove from skillet and serve on long wooden skewers or toothpicks and accompany with sauce.

TO PREPARE SAUCE: In a small saucepan over medium-high heat, bring tomato sauce, oil, and anchovy paste to a gentle boil.

Remove from heat and stir in breadcrumbs to thicken.

Serve croquettes with sauce.

Serves 8.

chickpea chat

Chickpeas (also called garbanzo beans) are often used in Mediterranean, Indian, and Middle Eastern dishes. These legumes are available canned and dried, and are popular in salads, soups, and stews.

APPROXIMATE PER SERVING: *130 calories; 3 grams of fat*

Summer Sparkler

1 10-ounce package frozen unsweetened strawberries
2 8-ounce cans crushed pineapple with juice
1-1/2 cups orange juice
1 quart carbonated water, chilled

Reserving 8 strawberries for garnish, combine strawberries with pineapple and its juice in a blender until smooth. Add orange juice.

Pour into ice cube trays and freeze.

Before serving, place three cubes into each of 8 tall glasses and fill each with carbonated water. Allow to melt slightly and become slushy.

Garnish each glass with a strawberry.

Makes 64 ounces.
Serves 8.

nice ice

Fill sections of ice cube trays with sliced strawberries and bottled water (which freezes into clear cubes), and serve guests drinks over fancy fruit cubes. Or for a fruit juice-based drink, freeze extra juice in ice cube trays and serve a drink that won't become diluted by water as ice cubes melt.

APPROXIMATE PER SERVING: *70 calories; 0 grams of fat*

Julienned Carrot and Celery Orzo

2 cups orzo, divided
1 teaspoon olive oil
1-1/2 quarts water
2 reduced sodium chicken bouillon cubes
4 stalks celery, julienned into 2-inch sticks
4 carrots, julienned into 2-inch sticks
1/2 teaspoon butter
Dash of pepper

In a medium saucepan over medium-high heat, brown 1 cup of orzo in olive oil, stirring constantly. Add water and bouillon cubes to saucepan and bring to a boil. Add remaining orzo and boil 5 minutes.

Add celery and carrots and boil an additional 4 minutes.

Drain well and mix in butter and pepper.

Serves 8.

just julienne

Before slicing round vegetables, cut a thin slice from the bottoms and set them on their flat edges so they won't roll. Slice vegetables into 1/8-inch-thick slices, stack them, then cut them into 1/8-inch-thick strips. Trim the strips into shorter pieces before using.

APPROXIMATE PER SERVING: *240 calories; 2 grams of fat*

Seared Sesame Scallops with Avocado Sauce

The fat in this dish comes mainly from the avocado. Avocados contain heart-healthy monounsaturated fat as well as vitamin C, thiamine, and riboflavin. Serving this dish alongside lower-fat dishes helps keep the menu's overall fat content at approximately 22%.

Scallops:
2 pounds sea scallops
1/2 cup sesame seeds
2 teaspoons olive oil
1/2 teaspoon garlic salt
2 large yellow peppers, seeded and sliced thinly
10 cups fresh spinach, loosely packed
1 teaspoon minced garlic

Sauce:
2 tablespoons lime juice
2 ripe avocados, mashed
1/2 teaspoon garlic salt
2 teaspoons cilantro
1 cup light sour cream

1/4 cup fresh cilantro to garnish

TO PREPARE SCALLOPS: In a small bowl coat scallops with sesame seeds.

In a large nonstick or cast-iron skillet, heat olive oil over medium-high heat.

Sear scallops for 1 to 2 minutes per side until slightly brown; sprinkle with garlic salt. Reduce heat to low and cook scallops 1 to 2 minutes longer, until just done. Do not overcook.

Remove scallops from pan and set aside.

Return pan to medium-high heat. Add yellow peppers to skillet and sauté until tender; remove and set aside.

Add spinach and garlic to pan and sauté until tender.

(continued on next page)

TO PREPARE SAUCE: Heat lime juice, avocados, garlic salt, and cilantro over medium heat until just warm. Do not bring to boil.

Stir in sour cream and heat until warm but not hot.

To serve, spread spinach on a medium platter and top with half of sauce. Top sauce with yellow peppers, scallops, and remaining sauce.

Sprinkle with cilantro.

Serves 8.

shelling out for scallops

Avoid bright white scallops. You'll be paying too much, as these have been soaked in water to increase their weight. Choose scallops that are pale beige to creamy pink in appearance. They should look moist, but not gummy, and have a sweet smell. Keep fresh scallops refrigerated and use within 2 days.

APPROXIMATE PER SERVING: *300 calories; 17 grams of fat*

Zucchini and Squash Tart

Crust:
2 cups plus 2 tablespoons reduced-fat baking mix, divided
1/2 cup 1% milk

Cooking spray

Filling:
1 cup skim milk ricotta cheese
1 tablespoon dry ranch salad dressing mix
1 large onion, sliced finely
1 medium crookneck squash, sliced into thin coins
1 medium zucchini, sliced into thin coins
1/4 cup part-skim mozzarella cheese
1 tablespoon imitation (soy) bacon bits

Preheat oven to 450°F.

TO PREPARE CRUST: Combine 2 cups of baking mix and milk in a small bowl.

Turn dough onto surface sprinkled with 2 tablespoons of baking mix and knead 10 times.

Coat an 8 × 8-inch pan with cooking spray and press dough into it, leaving a 1/2-inch crust around edges.

Bake for 8 to 9 minutes until lightly browned. Remove from oven and cool.

TO PREPARE FILLING: In a small bowl, stir together ricotta cheese and ranch dressing mix. Spread mixture on crust to edges.

Sauté onion in a small nonstick skillet until tender.

Spread onions on top of cheese mixture. Top with summer squash and zucchini coins. Sprinkle with mozzarella cheese and bacon bits.

Bake for 10 to 12 minutes until slightly brown and bubbling.

Serves 8.

squash talk

The most common varieties of summer squash in the U.S. are crookneck, zucchini, and pattypan. The flesh, which has a high water content and is easily bruised, has a mild flavor. Choose small squash with bright, unblemished skin. Refrigerate summer squash in a plastic bag for no more than 5 days. Summer squash are good sources of vitamin A, vitamin C, and niacin.

APPROXIMATE PER SERVING: *180 calories; 4 grams of fat*

Summer Strawberry Shortcake

Garnish the shortcakes with strawberries and/or mint leaves before serving.

3 pints strawberries, washed, hulled, and halved
2/3 cup strawberry preserves
1/3 cup honey
4 teaspoons lemon juice
4 cups low-fat whipped topping
1 loaf fat-free pound cake, sliced into 8 pieces

Set aside 1/3 pint of strawberries to use as a garnish.

Mix together strawberries, preserves, honey, and lemon juice in a medium bowl.

Place 1 slice of pound cake onto each dessert plate.

Spoon strawberry mixture over cake. Spread 2 tablespoons of whipped topping over mixture.

Place a second slice of pound cake over whipped topping. Spoon strawberry mixture over cake.

Finish with a dollop of whipped topping.

Serve immediately.

Serves 8.

strawberry?

Eight medium-sized strawberries contain 20 percent of the recommended daily allowance for folic acid and more Vitamin C than an orange. • On average, there are 200 tiny seeds in every strawberry. • The strawberry isn't a true berry. True berries have seeds inside. The strawberry, however, shows its "seeds" (each of which is actually considered a separate fruit) on the outside.

APPROXIMATE PER SERVING: *427 calories; 6 grams of fat*

NOTES

NOTES

Mount Olympus Greek Party

Throw this party to coincide with the summer or winter Olympics and invite friends over for the opening or closing ceremonies. Or just use this theme as an excuse to wear a toga. The Greek menu will get everyone in the spirit of the event!

menu for 8

- Heavenly Hummus
- Cucumber Yogurt Dip
- Nectar of the Gods
- Lemon Spinach Soup
- Greek Chicken with Tomatoes, Peppers, Olives, and Feta
- Rice with Orzo and Mint
- Greek Salad
- Baklava with Fruit Compote

Invitations

- Include the Olympic rings motif if you're coordinating your party with an Olympic broadcast. Don't forget to list the schedule of events for the night of the party in the invitation.

- Draw a simple border of laurel leaves or ivy around the edge of the invitation and write party details inside.

- SAMPLE WORDING: Please join us for the Opening Ceremonies of the Olympic Games • And take part in a Mini Olympics with Award Ceremony • Dress appropriately for Olympic events (togas optional)

Decorations

- Border a white tablecloth with gold fabric paint, arrange white garden columns on the table or at the entryway, and arrange bay leaves (also called laurel) or other cut foliage, grapes, figs, and nuts around serving pieces on the table.

- For a centerpiece, simply arrange white lilies in a round glass vase and tie with a golden tassel or circle with greenery. Or create a striking arrangement of frosted grapes. Dip small bunches of grapes into a mix of 2 packages of unflavored gelatin and 1/2 cup of white sugar. Gently shake off excess and set grapes on wax paper to dry. Arrange in a decorative bowl.

- Pin up travel posters of Greece and/or the city of the current Olympics.

Activity

- Hold a mini Olympics. Set up fun events for guests in the backyard, basement, or spare room, such as the javelin (banana toss), discus (tortilla throw), shot-put (orange-put), and chariot races (one person carried by two others chariot style). Give medals (foil-covered card board strung on ribbon) or other prizes to winners.

Setting the Scene

- Show the Olympic opening or closing ceremonies or event broadcast on television if applicable.

- For theme music for the party, consider playing:
  All-Time Greatest Hits by the R&B band the Olympics.

- Or for fun, contemporary Greek music, listen to Greek folk music or a combination of Greek music and dance music, respectively:
  Di Efchon by Haris Alexiou
  Greek Fire by Annabouboula

Heavenly Hummus

Hummus is traditionally made with tahini, a high-fat paste made from sesame seeds. But you'll never know it's missing from this recipe. Serve hummus with pita chips.

3 garlic cloves
1/4 cup plain low-fat yogurt
1 tablespoon fresh lemon juice
1 teaspoon olive oil
1/4 teaspoon salt
1/4 teaspoon paprika
1/8 teaspoon pepper
1 19-ounce can chickpeas, drained

Turn on food processor and drop garlic in food chute. Process until minced finely.

Add yogurt and remaining ingredients while processor is still on. Process until smooth.

Makes approximately 2 cups.
Serves 8.

quick and easy pita chips

Split pita bread and cut into bite-sized pieces. Arrange pita pieces on a cookie sheet and broil for 6 to 8 minutes, watching carefully to prevent overcooking. When pita is golden brown, remove from broiler.

APPROXIMATE PER SERVING: *80 calories; 1.7 grams of fat*

Cucumber Yogurt Dip

This dip will get watery if it sits several hours, so serve it at once. Accompany the dip with crudités, such as sticks of carrots, celery, and peppers.

2-1/2 medium cucumbers, chilled, peeled, cut into 1/2-inch cubes
1/3 cup parsley, chopped
3 scallions, chopped finely
1/4 teaspoon garlic salt
1 teaspoon lemon juice
1 teaspoon oregano
4 dashes black pepper
2/3 cup light cream cheese, softened

Mix cucumbers, parsley, and scallions in a bowl. Stir in garlic salt, lemon juice, oregano, and pepper.

Stir in cream cheese.

Serve immediately.

Makes approximately 2-1/2 cups.
Serves 8 with crudités.

cool as a cucumber

The cucumber is originally from southern Asia. Mature cucumbers contain larger and more bitter seeds than younger cucumbers, so choose tender young vegetables or remove the seeds from older cucumbers before eating them.

APPROXIMATE PER SERVING: *39 calories; 2 grams of fat*

Nectar of the Gods

Sugar syrup, or simple syrup, is a mixture of sugar and water cooked over low heat until the sugar is dissolved, then boiled for a minute or so. For this drink, combine 1/4 cup of sugar with 3/4 cup of water to allow for the water that will boil off.

1/2 cup sugar syrup
1 cup lemon juice
2 cups strong green tea
1 quart white grape juice
1 block ice
1 quart chilled club soda

In a large punch bowl combine all ingredients except soda and ice block.

Refrigerate for an hour or two.

Add ice block to the punch. Gently pour the soda over the punch and ice.

Makes approximately 11-1/2 cups.
Serves 8.

lemon cubes

For beautiful ice cubes, place a small lemon slice, sliced grape, mint sprig, or other sliced fruit or herb sprig in each section of an ice cube tray. Add bottled water (which will freeze into clear cubes) and freeze. Serve drink over cubes.

APPROXIMATE PER SERVING: *62 calories; 0 grams of fat*

Lemon Spinach Soup

2 medium onions, sliced lengthwise into 1/2-inch strips
1-1/3 teaspoon olive oil
8 cups fat-free chicken broth
1/3 cup fresh lemon juice
7 cups fresh spinach, packed down, washed
Dash of pepper (to taste)
1 lemon, sliced paper thin

In a medium stockpot, sauté onion in oil over medium-high heat until tender.

Add chicken broth and lemon juice. Stir in spinach, reduce heat, and simmer 5 minutes.

Season with pepper if desired.

Serve hot with lemon slices floating on top.

Serves 8.

popeye's favorite

Spinach is a rich source of iron as well as vitamins A and C. Fresh spinach is usually gritty, so wash it thoroughly. Add a small amount of salt to cold water, rinse the spinach in it, and rinse and drain in a colander. Pat dry.

APPROXIMATE PER SERVING: *44 calories; 1 gram of fat*

Greek Chicken with Tomatoes, Peppers, Olives, and Feta

To make Greek seasoning salt, combine 2 teaspoons of garlic salt, 2 teaspoons of lemon pepper, 2 teaspoons of oregano, and 2 teaspoons of dried mint.

4 boneless, skinless chicken breast halves, cut into bite-sized pieces
1/4 cup flour
8 teaspoons Greek seasoning salt, divided
1 teaspoon olive oil
1 large onion, sliced lengthwise
1 green pepper, cored, seeded, and sliced lengthwise into strips
3 Roma tomatoes, cut into eighths
3 tablespoons Kalamata olives, chopped
3 tablespoons feta cheese, crumbled

Dredge chicken in flour mixed with 4 teaspoons of Greek seasoning.

Heat oil in a large skillet over medium heat and add chicken, sautéing for 3 to 4 minutes until cooked through.

Remove chicken from pan and set aside.

Add onion to skillet and sauté until tender, about 2 minutes. Add bell pepper and cook another 2 minutes.

Return chicken to skillet and cook 1 to 2 minutes, sprinkling with remaining Greek seasoning. Mix in tomatoes.

Remove from heat, transfer to serving dish, and sprinkle with olives and feta cheese.

Serves 8.

chilly tomatoes

Don't put tomatoes in the refrigerator. They ripen and remain flavorful at room temperature. Use ripe tomatoes within 3 days.

APPROXIMATE PER SERVING: *210 calories; 9.5 grams of fat*

Rice with Orzo and Mint

1/2 cup orzo
1 teaspoon olive oil
3 cups fat-free chicken broth
1-1/3 cups uncooked brown rice
1/2 teaspoon garlic salt
3 tablespoons fresh mint

In a medium saucepan on medium-high heat, brown orzo in olive oil, stirring constantly. Pour in chicken broth and bring to boil.

Add rice and garlic salt and return to boil. Reduce heat and simmer 45 minutes. Remove from heat and stir in fresh mint.

Serves 8.

use orzo instead

Orzo is a tiny, rice-shaped pasta. It's great in soups and is a wonderful pasta substitute for rice.

APPROXIMATE PER SERVING: *149 calories; 2 grams of fat*

Greek Salad

2 heads curly leaf lettuce
2 cups seeded, diced, peeled cucumber
2 cups seeded, diced red bell pepper
2 cups seeded, diced green bell pepper
4 ounces crumbled feta cheese (approximately 1 cup)
1/2 cup diced red onion
1/2 cup chopped pepperoncini peppers
1/2 cup Kalamata olives, pitted and chopped
1/4 cup lemon juice
4 teaspoons dried oregano
2 teaspoons extra-virgin olive oil
1/2 teaspoon ground white pepper

Combine all ingredients in a large bowl; toss gently.

Serves 8.

fabulous feta

Feta cheese is a Greek cheese classically made with sheep's or goat's milk, although today it is often made with cow's milk. With a crumbly texture and tangy taste, feta is popular as an addition to salads as well as cooked dishes. It contains from 45 to 60 percent milk fat.

APPROXIMATE PER SERVING: *95 calories; 4 grams of fat*

Baklava with Fruit Compote

Baklava is a rich dessert usually made with butter, nuts—both high in fat—honey, and sugar. Our lightened version offers a full, nutty flavor and omits the butter. Its delicious flavor will have your guests clamoring for more!

Baklava:
3/4 cup chopped pecans
1/4 cup chopped pistachio nuts
1/4 cup sesame seeds
1/8 cup honey
1-1/4 teaspoons lemon juice
1-1/4 teaspoons cinnamon
3 sheets phyllo dough

Fruit compote:
1/4 cup orange juice
1/4 cup apple juice
1/4 cup honey
2 small apples, peeled, cored, and cut into wedges
Powdered sugar and cinnamon for garnish

Preheat oven to 400°F.

TO PREPARE BAKLAVA: Mix pecans, pistachios, sesame seeds, honey, lemon juice, and cinnamon in a bowl.

Gently unwrap phyllo dough from its package so that it lies flat. Using a sharp knife, cut the phyllo into 5 × 5-inch pieces, totaling 16 pieces. Stack 2 pieces of phyllo on top of each other to form 8 squares.

Spread approximately 1 tablespoon of nut mixture in center of each square of phyllo. Bring corners of dough together and pinch above nut mixture to seal. Set each phyllo packet on a lightly greased cookie sheet.

Bake for 10 minutes or until golden brown. Set aside.

TO PREPARE FRUIT COMPOTE: Combine juices, honey, and apples in a saucepan. Simmer 5 to 10 minutes or until apples are tender.

Spoon warm fruit compote over each piece of baklava and serve immediately.

Makes approximately 12 cups.
Serves 8.

APPROXIMATE PER SERVING: *187 calories; 8 grams of fat*

NOTES

Country Fair Canning Party

This celebration of the harvest is a wonderful reason for friends and family to exchange recipes, can items together, and share a meal. Plan your Country Fair Canning Party during September or another time when garden harvests are fresh.

Because canning is a very time-consuming, labor-intensive, and often messy endeavor, we've suggested alternative activities as well. You may choose to entertain your guests in a different way—especially if you have a small kitchen.

menu for 8

- Blue Ribbon Sun-Dried Tomato Dip
- Caramel Dipping Sauce
- Mulled Punch
- Farm-Fresh Deviled Eggs
- Creamy Double-O Relish
- Country Coleslaw
- Harvest Ham Primavera
- Blueberry Peach Crisp

Invitations

- Cover card stock with red or blue gingham. Glue a canning jar lid to it and write the party information on top. Be sure to use the largest lids available so there's enough room to write in party particulars.

- For a simpler invitation, cut gingham frames with pinking shears to fit around the card stock. Glue the gingham frame to the edge of the card stock.

- Ask guests to bring produce to can and glass canning jars, or simply ask them to bring copies of their favorite recipes for swapping.

Decorations

- Cover the table with a red or blue gingham tablecloth and napkins tied with twine.

- Fill large and small canning jars, new or antique, with garden flowers. Use small canning jars as drink glasses. Fill wooden bushel barrels and produce baskets with fresh fruits and vegetables like blueberries, peaches, tomatoes, green beans, etc.

- Set out cornucopias for a touch of fall.

Activities

- CANNING: Enjoy the fruits of your labor and preserve garden harvests (or fresh items from a local farm stand or farmer's market). Guests may also work together to can produce or special recipes like pasta sauce or vegetable soup.

  You may find it helpful to set up stations at the stove, counter, sink, and table. The stove station can be used for boiling cans and lids, as well as cooking any ingredients. (Be prepared to provide a large pan or any other necessary items; you may wish to ask your guests to bring main ingredients from their recipe.) The counter station can be occupied for cutting or processing and the sink station can be used for peeling, coring, cleaning, and so on. Use the table station as a workspace for creating labels.

Provide decorating supplies for labels such as scraps of fabric, pinking shears, ribbons, labels, raffia, paper tags, and glue guns. Encourage guests to swap cans so everyone goes home with a variety of canned items.

- CAN AND RECIPE SWAP: Ask guests to bring already-canned fresh produce or jellies and favorite recipes to the party and allow them to exchange canned items and recipes.

- HARVESTING: Take a day trip to a local farmer's market, orchard, or garden where people may choose produce to can (at a later time). After returning, invite guests to swap recipes and troubleshooting tips for their canning experience at home.

- APPLE TASTING: Purchase different varieties of apples at the farmer's market. Set up an apple tasting area. Cut apples into slices, coating with lemon juice or fruit freshening powder to keep from browning, label, and have guests try each kind. Serve with Caramel Dipping Sauce (recipe appears in this theme).

Setting the Scene

- Play good old country music to get guests in the mood for the hard work of canning or as background music for swapping and discussing canned goods and recipes:
  Patsy Cline's *Greatest Hits*
  Rockin' Country Party Pack by Confederate Railroad
  Tribute to Tradition by various country artists
  Appalachian Stomp: Bluegrass Classics by various artists

Blue Ribbon Sun-Dried Tomato Dip

1 3-ounce package sun-dried tomatoes, packed without oil (about 2 cups)
1 cup water
1/3 cup fresh basil leaves (do not substitute dried basil)
2 tablespoons balsamic vinegar
2 tablespoons Italian-style tomato paste
1 tablespoon olive oil
1/8 teaspoon salt
1/8 teaspoon pepper
1 15-ounce can white beans, drained
1 garlic clove, minced
4 whole-wheat pitas

TO PREPARE DIP: Bring 1 cup of water to a boil. In a medium bowl, combine dried tomatoes and boiling water. Let stand for at least 15 minutes. Drain tomatoes, reserving 1/2 cup of soaking water.

In a food processor, blend softened tomatoes, reserved water, fresh basil, and remaining ingredients (vinegar through garlic); process until smooth.

TO PREPARE PITA CHIPS: Cut pita bread into bite-sized chips, separating the bread where the pocket would be.

Arrange pieces on a cookie sheet and broil for 4 to 6 minutes, watching carefully. When pita is golden brown, remove from broiler. Serve with dip.

Makes approximately 2-1/2 cups.
Serves 8.

sun-dried tomatoes

Sun drying results in a chewy, intensely flavored, sweet yet slightly salty dark red tomato. Dried tomatoes need to be reconstituted before use. You soak the dried tomatoes in hot water, broth, wine, or other cooking liquid; reserve the liquid, and use it to add flavor to stocks and sauces. • A package of unopened, commercially dried tomatoes can be stored at room temperature for six to nine months; refrigerate or freeze after opening.

APPROXIMATE PER SERVING: *21 calories; 0.6 grams of fat*

Caramel Dipping Sauce

Serve this sauce with a selection of apple varieties, cut into slices. Try Rome, Granny Smith, Golden or Red Delicious, Braeburn, Gala, and Fuji.

3/4 cup sugar
1/3 cup water
2 tablespoons light butter
1 ounce 1/3-less-fat cream cheese (Neufchâtel) (about 2 tablespoons)
1/4 cup 1% low-fat milk
2 teaspoons imitation rum extract

In a small saucepan, cook sugar and water, stirring constantly over medium-high heat until sugar dissolves.

Cook, without stirring, until golden for an additional 15 minutes.

Remove from heat.

Stir constantly with a wire whisk as butter and cream cheese are added to caramelized sugar. (Mixture will be very hot and bubbly.)

Allow to cool slightly. Stir in milk and rum extract.

Serve with apple slices of your choice.

Makes approximately 1-1/2 cups.
Serves 8.

apple facts

1. Apples are the second most purchased fruit, ranking below bananas. 2. Tens of thousands of varieties of apples are grown throughout the world. 3. Do not store apples next to strong-smelling vegetables or fruits, as they will pick up the smell and flavor of those products. 4. Avoid storing apples next to items that you do not want to ripen further. Apples release ethylene gas that will ripen other produce such as tomatoes, peaches, or pears. 5. In ancient Greece, if a man tossed an apple to a woman, it indicated a proposal of marriage; if she caught it, it meant that she accepted.

APPROXIMATE PER SERVING: *204 calories; 4.5 grams of fat*

Mulled Punch

This warm punch will make your whole home smell delicious!

4 cups cranberry-raspberry drink
2 cups orange-strawberry-banana juice
1 teaspoon whole allspice
2 orange-and-spice tea bags
5 3 × 3/4-inch lemon rind strips
1 3-inch cinnamon stick
1/4 cup sweetened dried cranberries
1/4 cup diced dried apricots
2 tablespoons sugar
Cinnamon sticks (optional)

Pour the juices into a large saucepan or Dutch oven.

Add allspice, tea bags, lemon rinds, and cinnamon sticks to the liquid. Simmer the mixture for 30 minutes over medium-low heat.

Remove from heat; allow to cool for 30 minutes. Strain mixture. Discard solids and return juice mixture to pan.

Add the dried fruits and sugar to the juice mixture. Simmer over medium-low heat for 30 minutes, stirring occasionally.

Ladle into mugs. Serve warm and garnish with a cinnamon stick, if desired.

Makes approximately 6 cups.
Serves 8.

mull it over

Mulling is the process of flavoring a beverage by heating it and adding herbs, spices, fruit, and sugar.

APPROXIMATE PER SERVING: *151 calories; 0.1 grams of fat*

Farm-Fresh Deviled Eggs

Boil the eggs in vinegar to keep the egg white intact in case the eggs leak or break during boiling.

8 large eggs
1 teaspoon white vinegar
4 tablespoons light mayonnaise
1/2 teaspoon dry mustard
2 teaspoons Worcestershire sauce
1/2 teaspoon hot pepper sauce, or to taste
Dash of paprika
1 tablespoon fresh parsley, chopped finely

Place eggs and vinegar in a medium saucepan, cover with water, and bring to boil. Reduce heat and boil gently for 10 minutes.

Remove from heat and cool.

Peel eggs and cut in half lengthwise. Scoop out yolks and put in a small bowl. Transfer whites to a serving tray.

Mash yolks with a fork. Blend in mayonnaise, mustard, Worcestershire sauce, hot pepper sauce, and paprika.

Fill each egg white half with yolk mixture and sprinkle with parsley.

Serves 8.

fresh egg test

To test eggs for freshness, place eggs in a pot of water. Older eggs will float, while fresh eggs stay at the bottom.

APPROXIMATE PER SERVING: *100 calories; 8 grams of fat*

Creamy Double-O Relish

Serve this relish with whole-wheat crackers.

1 8-ounce package fat-free cream cheese, softened
1 tablespoon sugar
2 large oranges, peeled and diced
1 medium red onion, diced finely
1/2 teaspoon orange zest, slivered
1 tablespoon cornstarch dissolved in 1 tablespoon orange juice
24 whole-wheat crackers

Wrap cream cheese in plastic wrap and shape into a flattened circle. Chill.

In a small saucepan over medium heat, bring oranges, onions, sugar, and 1/4 teaspoon of orange zest to a boil. Add cornstarch mixture and cook until thickened.

Remove from heat, transfer to a small bowl, and chill.

To serve, remove plastic wrap from cream cheese and position on serving plate. Spoon relish over cream cheese and sprinkle with remaining zest.

Serve with whole-wheat crackers.

Makes approximately 1 cup.
Serves 8.

zest for food

The outermost, colored skin layer of a citrus fruit is called the zest. The flavor arises from the aromatic oils in the skin. A special kitchen utensil called a citrus zester can remove the perfumy skin, but a paring knife or vegetable peeler also work well. Avoid the white pith as it can taste bitter.

APPROXIMATE PER SERVING: *110 calories; 2.5 grams of fat*

Country Coleslaw

Dressing:
1/3 cup granulated sugar
1/2 teaspoon salt
Dash of pepper
1/4 cup skim milk
1/2 cup light mayonnaise
1/4 cup nonfat buttermilk
1-1/2 tablespoons white vinegar
2-1/2 tablespoons lemon juice

Slaw:
1/2 head white cabbage, finely shredded
1/2 head purple cabbage, finely shredded
2 tablespoons finely minced onion
1/4 cup finely shredded carrot

Whisk dressing ingredients in a large bowl.

Combine shredded vegetables with dressing. Refrigerate for at least 2 hours before serving.

Serves 8.

food that fights cancer

Cabbage is a cruciferous vegetable. Research has shown that cruciferous vegetables may protect against certain cancers.

APPROXIMATE PER SERVING: *110 calories; 5 grams of fat*

Harvest Ham Primavera

Choose crisp, bright green snow peas with small seeds. Remember to cut off the tips at both ends before using.

1 16-ounce box pound bowtie pasta (farfalle)
1 teaspoon olive oil
8-ounce ham steak, trimmed well, cooked and cut into 1-inch cubes
1 medium red onion, sliced finely
1 medium yellow pepper, sliced finely
1/4-pound snow peas, blanched in hot water for 1 minute
2 Roma tomatoes, diced
1 cup 1% milk
1 tablespoon onion and chive fat-free cream cheese
1 tablespoon cornstarch dissolved in 1 tablespoon 1% milk
2 tablespoons Parmesan cheese, grated, divided
2 tablespoons chives, chopped
Cooking spray

In a large stockpot, cook pasta according to package directions. Drain pasta, return to pot, and stir in olive oil.

Add ham steak cubes to pasta and cover to keep warm.

In a large skillet that has been lightly sprayed with cooking spray, sauté onion until tender. Add yellow pepper and snow peas, cook 1 minute, and add to pasta.

snow peas

Why are snow peas called snow peas? They are grown all year long with peak harvesting seasons in the spring and fall. The French name for snow pea is mange-tout, translated as "eat it all." This name comes from the fact that the entire legume—pod and all—can be consumed.

Mix tomatoes into hot pasta.

In same skillet over medium-high heat, bring milk to a gentle boil. Stir in cream cheese until it melts. Add cornstarch mixture and 1 tablespoon of Parmesan cheese. Cook 1 to 2 minutes more, or until thickened. Pour over pasta mixture and stir gently until mixed thoroughly.

Transfer to heated serving dish. Top with remaining Parmesan cheese and chopped chives.

Serves 8.

APPROXIMATE PER SERVING: *250 calories; 4 grams of fat*

Blueberry Peach Crisp

6 cups fresh peaches, peeled and sliced
2 cups fresh blueberries
1/3 cup plus 1/4 cup light brown sugar, divided
2 tablespoons all-purpose flour
1 tablespoon cinnamon, divided
1 cup quick-cooking oats
3 tablespoons margarine

Preheat oven to 350°F.

In a 2-quart baking dish, combine peaches and blueberries.

Combine 1/3 cup of brown sugar, flour, and 2 teaspoons of cinnamon in a small bowl and mix well. Add to peaches and blueberries, tossing to mix.

Combine oats, 1/4 cup of brown sugar, and 1 teaspoon of cinnamon in a bowl.

With a pastry blender or fork, cut in margarine until crumbly, then sprinkle over fruit.

Bake for 25 minutes or until fruit is just tender and mixture is bubbly.

Serves 8.

peak harvest Blueberries and peaches both peak in July; however, both fruits are available until September.

APPROXIMATE PER SERVING: *203 calories; 5 grams of fat*

NOTES

NOTES

Pre-Hike Breakfast

This power-packed breakfast is great to enjoy with active friends before a day of hiking at a local park or hiking trail. It's easy for the host or hostess, too—it features Make-Your-Own-Cereal and On-the-Trail-Mix for the outing. Plan your hike to coincide with a time of year when leaves are changing or flowers are blooming and the weather is mild.

menu for 8

- Energizing Smoothie
- Glorious Fruit Salad
- Sparkling Sunset Citrus Spritzer
- Rise 'n Shine English Muffins
- Breakfast Burritos
- Pumpkin Oat Muffins
- Make-Your-Own-Cereal and On-the-Trail Mix

Invitations

- Obtain an old map (one that has been updated or outlived its usefulness), a new map from a convenience store, or a map downloaded from the Internet and printed with a color printer. Cut the map into 6 × 4-inch pieces. Cut card stock into 3 × 5-inch pieces and paste it onto the map pieces. Write party information and activities on the card stock.

- SAMPLE WORDING: Get your heart going with a group hike! Please meet at Jeff's at 8 AM Saturday to assemble a yummy breakfast and trail snacks. The hike up the ridge will take 2 hours round-trip.

- Include a photocopied map of the location of where you plan to hike, such as a local hiking trail, a mountain, or waterfalls.

Decorations

- Set the scene with a tablecloth with a nature theme, such as a pattern of leaves, acorns, or pinecones.

- Use natural baskets lined with clear bowls to hold food.

- A tall, rustic basket filled with wildflowers or leaves from the backyard can be used as an easy and interesting centerpiece.

Activities

- PERSONALIZE YOUR TRAIL MIX BAG: Set up a Make-Your-Own cereal/Trail Mix area by filling various sized bowls with cereal/trail mix ingredients and small scoops or large spoons. Give each guest a large cereal bowl to fill for breakfast. Serve with milk. Provide your guests with paper lunch bags (or resealable plastic bags) to fill with their own combination of On-the-Trail Mix. Use twine to close the paper bags securely.

- Invite your guests to decorate their Trail Mix paper bags before filling them. Place magic markers, crayons, construction paper, glue, water paints, and other creative items nearby so that each person can personalize their trail mix bag.

- HIT THE TRAIL: Map out a trail in a local hiking or recreational area or simply hit the trail and determine your route as you go. Remember to tell a neighbor or friend where your group is hiking and when you plan to return.

Setting the Scene

- Play upbeat pop or rock to get guests inspired before their morning hike. Some possibilities:
  Hits by Phil Collins
  The Greatest Hits Vol. 1:20 Good Vibrations by the Beach Boys
  Ricky Martin by Ricky Martin
  Vacation by the Go Go's

Energizing Smoothie

This tofu drink is packed with calcium, vitamin C, potassium, and fiber, so it's a drink that will give you a boost any time of the day. Tofu is also a great source of soy.

1-1/2 cups sliced ripe banana (approximately 3 bananas)
1-1/2 cups frozen sweetened sliced strawberries, partially thawed
1-1/2 cups soft silken tofu, drained (about 3 ounces)
1-1/2 cups low-fat vanilla yogurt

Combine all ingredients in a blender or food processor and process until smooth.

Makes approximately 5 cups.
Serves 8.

the joy of soy

Isoflavones in soy may have protective effects against breast and prostate cancer. Studies on individual soy components are currently underway.

APPROXIMATE PER SERVING: *180 calories; 2 grams of fat*

Glorious Fruit Salad

Make this fruit salad the day before the hike to save yourself time in the morning.

1/4 cup fresh lime juice
1/4 cup honey
1/4 cup chopped fresh mint
1 3-pound cantaloupe, halved, seeded
1 12-ounce basket strawberries, hulled, halved
4 kiwis, peeled, cut into 1/2-inch pieces
1 1/2 cups seedless grapes

In a small bowl, whisk together lime juice, honey, and mint. Set aside.

Using a melon baller, scoop out cantaloupe into a large bowl. Add strawberries, kiwis, and grapes.

Pour syrup on the top of the prepared fruit and toss to coat. Let stand at least 15 minutes for flavors to combine.

Cover and chill if not serving immediately.

Serves 8.

what's in that fruit salad?

Ellagic acid is a compound found in raspberries, grapes, and other plant foods that may help reduce cancer risk. How deliciously healthy!

APPROXIMATE PER SERVING: *137 calories; 1 gram of fat*

Sparkling Sunset Citrus Spritzer

Try this refreshing cool drink after your long hike on the trail!

2-1/2 cups fresh orange juice (about 8 oranges)
1-1/2 cups fresh tangerine juice (about 6 tangerines)
1 25.4-ounce bottle sparkling apple cider, chilled
1/4 cup grenadine

Use cheesecloth to strain orange and tangerine juices into a large bowl or pitcher. Discard seeds and pulp.

Combine juices and cider and stir well.

Pour 3/4 cup into each of 8 glasses.

Slowly pour 1-1/2 teaspoons of grenadine down the inside of each glass. Do not stir before serving.

Serves 8.

an idea for citrus peels

The next time you use a lemon, lime, orange, or any other citrus fruit, instead of throwing away the rind, wash and grate it. Keep it in a container in the fridge. Add it to a favorite dish such as a dip, dessert, or meat for an extra dash of flavor, or add a little to steeping tea. Throw the rest of the rind in the disposal for a sweet-smelling sink.

APPROXIMATE PER SERVING: *102 calories; 0.2 grams of fat*

Rise 'n Shine English Muffins

12 ounces fresh mushrooms, sliced (or 4 to 4-1/2 cups)
2 cups green bell pepper, seeded and chopped
2 cups yellow onion, chopped
Egg substitute equivalent to 5 eggs, or 3 large eggs and whites of 3 large eggs
3/4 cup fat-free milk
3/4 cup no-salt-added tomato sauce
3 teaspoons salt-free dried Italian seasoning, crumbled
1/2 teaspoon crushed red pepper flakes
4 English muffins, halved and toasted
1/4 cup grated Parmesan cheese
Vegetable cooking spray

Heat a large nonstick pan over medium-high for 1 minute. Lightly coat with cooking spray.

Add mushrooms to the pan and sauté mushrooms until soft, about 4 minutes. Add bell pepper and onion and sauté the mixture for 4 to 5 minutes, or until onion is translucent.

(continued on next page)

salt is tough on eggs

Salt added to eggs causes them to toughen. It can also cause fried or scrambled eggs to stick to the pan. So add salt to your egg dish after preparation rather than while it's cooking.

As the ingredients in the skillet are cooking, whisk together eggs and milk in a small bowl.

Reduce heat to medium and add egg mixture to vegetables. Cook until eggs are set, stirring occasionally with a spatula.

Remove from heat.

Meanwhile, combine tomato sauce, Italian seasoning, and red pepper flakes in a small bowl. Spread approximately 2 tablespoons of tomato mixture on each muffin half.

Top with vegetable/egg mixture and sprinkle with Parmesan cheese.

Serves 8.

APPROXIMATE PER SERVING: *177 calories; 3 grams of fat*

Breakfast Burritos

Scrambling eggs with club soda (or adding 1/4 teaspoon of cornstarch per egg) makes them lighter, fluffier, and tastier!

Beans:

2 15-ounce cans pinto beans, undrained

2 4-ounce can chiles, chopped, undrained

1/4 teaspoon cumin

1/4 teaspoon chili powder

1/2 teaspoon minced onion

Dash hot pepper sauce, or to taste

Eggs:

Egg substitute equivalent to 6 eggs, or 4 large eggs and whites of 4 large eggs

1/4 cup club soda

Dash of salt

8 whole-wheat tortillas

1/2 cup reduced fat cheddar cheese, shredded

6 tablespoons fat-free sour cream

2 cups salsa

1 teaspoon pickled jalapeños (optional)

Cooking spray

TO PREPARE BEANS: In a medium saucepan over medium-high heat, bring beans, chiles, cumin, chili powder, onion, and hot pepper sauce to a boil.

Reduce heat and simmer 10 to 15 minutes.

(continued on next page)

egg substitutes

Egg substitutes are lower in calories than eggs and are cholesterol free. They can be substituted for regular eggs in most recipes (except for some specialty desserts and baked goods).

TO PREPARE EGGS: Whisk eggs and club soda in a small bowl.

Preheat a large skillet; coat lightly with cooking spray. Pour in egg mixture and scramble. Season with salt.

TO PREPARE BURRITOS: Spoon a divided portion of eggs, beans, cheese, sour cream, and salsa onto each tortilla. Roll burrito-style and place in small baking dish lightly coated with cooking spray.

Top tortillas with remaining beans, salsa, cheese, and jalapeños if desired.

Broil until cheese melts. Remove from broiler, cool slightly and serve.

Serves 8.

APPROXIMATE PER SERVING: *202 calories; 1 gram of fat*

Pumpkin Oat Muffins

Any leftover Pumpkin Oat Muffins freeze well.

6 cups oat cereal flakes
2 teaspoons salt
1 cup sugar
5 cups whole-wheat flour
5 teaspoons baking soda
1 tablespoon dried ground ginger
1 tablespoon cinnamon
1 cup golden raisins
2 eggs, beaten
1 15-ounce can pumpkin
2 teaspoons vanilla
1 quart low-fat buttermilk
3/4 cup canola oil
Paper muffin cups

Preheat oven to 400°F.

Line 3 muffin pans with paper muffin cups.

In a large bowl, mix together cereal, salt, sugar, flour, baking soda, ginger, and cinnamon. Stir in raisins.

In a separate bowl, combine eggs, pumpkin, vanilla, buttermilk, and oil. Stir until blended.

Mix wet ingredients with dry until batter just holds together. Do not overmix.

Spoon batter into muffin cups (about 2/3 full). Bake for 17 minutes.

Makes 40 muffins.
Serves 8.

make your muffins tops

Be kind to your muffins—beat them no more than 15 seconds. Overbeating results in muffins that have a tough texture and the possibility of tunnels in the middle.

APPROXIMATE PER SERVING: *158 calories; 5 grams of fat*

Make-Your-Own Cereal and On-the-Trail Mix

Cereal suggestions:
O-shaped cereal
Bran, Rice, or Wheat Chex
Granola
Cracklin' Oat Bran

Fruit suggestions:
Raisins or golden raisins
Banana chips
Dates
Prunes
Other dried fruit, such as cranberries, blueberries, apricots, pineapple, apples, and papaya

Other suggestions:
Almonds
Peanuts
Walnuts
M&M candy
Coconut slices
Chocolate chips
Carob chips
Bite-sized pretzels
Marshmallows

Present various ingredients in different bowls or containers.

For the cereal, give each person a bowl and allow guests to choose the items for their cereal. Serve with skim or low-fat milk.

For trail mix, offer same items and brown paper bags or resealable plastic bags for guests to make trail mix. Shake gently to distribute ingredients.

cereal (Cereals are packed with energy-providing carbohydrates. Choose whole-grain cereal for a high-fiber boost to your diet.

Calories and fat will vary depending on ingredients and serving size.

NOTES

NOTES

Pumpkin-Carving Contest

This theme creates a fun way for friends, family, and neighbors to carve pumpkins together in preparation for Halloween. It's also a celebration of the beauty of autumn and the changing of the seasons. You may want to hold this event outdoors on a sunny fall afternoon, as the activities tend to get messy.

menu for 8

- Scary Spiced Popcorn
- Turkey Sausage Bites with Sweet Hot Mustard Sauce
- Hot Spiced Cider
- Herb-Rubbed Pork Loin with Apricot-Pecan Stuffing
- Spinach Soufflé
- Harvest Rice
- Pumpkin Mousse

Invitations

- Cut tan, orange, deep red, or other autumn-colored card stock into leaf shapes or decorate card stock with a leaf-imprinted rubber stamp. Cut out leaves of multiple shapes and sizes and punch holes through the top of the leaves. Tie the leaves together by threading natural raffia ribbon through the punched holes and tying. Write party information on the top leaf or on different leaves.

- SAMPLE WORDING: Please join us for a Pumpkin Carving and Autumn Feast on Saturday. B.Y.O.P. (Bring Your Own Pumpkin) and a knife or other utensils for the carving contest

Decorations

- Set up burlap tablecloths in fall colors of tan, gold, olive green, burgundy, or orange. If those prove difficult to find, use fabric paint to add color to natural burlap that has been cut to size. Make a stunning centerpiece using mums placed in top-cut pumpkins.

- Use terra cotta planters and natural baskets (lined with glass dishes if necessary) to hold food.

- Weather permitting, decorate an outdoor area with bales of hay; pumpkins and gourds; grapevine wreaths; and different baskets or bushel baskets filled with apples, Indian corn, wheat, squash, or other colorful fall vegetables.

- Wrap cornstalks around a light post, mailbox, tall birdfeeder, or other posts. Place sprigs of bittersweet in pumpkins or in a wreath for a welcoming door.

Activities

- PUMPKIN CARVING: Set up tables outside (weather permitting) covered with brown craft paper where adults can carve pumpkins. Afterward, as dusk sets, set the pumpkins out on the front porch or on a table. Illuminate them with candles and have guests vote for different categories, such as funniest, scariest, and most original.

  Provide acetone (fingernail polish remover) to remove magic marker, paper towels, matches or a lighter, serving spoons to scoop out seeds, and a large bowl to collect seeds.

- LEAF RAKING: Give children brown paper bags to store collected fall leaves. You might want to have a leaf-raking contest—set up bags for teams to place raked leaves in. The team with the heaviest bag wins. (The best part is that your yard gets raked!)

- APPLE BOBBING: Using a galvanized aluminum tub (available at many garden or hardware stores), set up an apple bobbing area. Remember to have towels handy!

- SCARECROWS: Provide kids with hay and old clothes so they can make a scarecrow.

Setting the Scene

- Tranquil music, such as classical or folk, elicits memories of cooler and shorter autumn days. In these styles, musical themes reflecting the seasons have been chosen often by artists as a creative backdrop. Some suggestions:
  "*Autumn*" from *The Four Seasons* by Vivaldi
  Meditations for Autumn by Brahms, Barber, Chopin, and others
  Autumn Songs—Popular Works for Solo Piano by John O'Conor
  Autumn by George Winston
  Sunday in Autumn by Jon Mark
  When October Goes—Autumn Love Songs by various folk artists

Scary Spiced Popcorn

1/4 cup margarine or reduced fat margarine, melted
1 teaspoon paprika
1/2 teaspoon crushed red pepper
1/2 teaspoon ground cumin
10 cups warm popped popcorn
1/3 cup grated Parmesan cheese

Pour melted butter into a small bowl. Measure in paprika, red pepper, and cumin and mix well.

Sprinkle the butter mixture over the popcorn and toss gently until coated evenly.

Sprinkle with Parmesan cheese and toss until coated.

Makes 10 cups.
Serves 8.

kernels of wisdom

Popcorn is a special variety of dried corn that bursts open and expands when heated. Natural moisture trapped inside the hull, when heated, evaporates and creates so much pressure that it explodes. • Store fresh popping corn at room temperature for up to one year. Popcorn stored in an airtight container will produce larger popped kernels, due to a loss of moisture.

APPROXIMATE PER SERVING: *82 calories; 3 grams of fat*

Turkey Sausage Bites with Sweet Hot Mustard Sauce

Sausage bites:

1-1/4 cups turkey breakfast sausage (patties or links with casings removed)
1 teaspoon canola oil
1 small onion, diced finely
1/2 green pepper, cored, seeded, and diced finely
1 cup reduced-fat baking mix
1/4 cup skim or 1% milk
1/2 teaspoon Dijon mustard
1/2 teaspoon honey
1/2 teaspoon garlic salt

Sauce:

1/4 cup honey
2 teaspoons Dijon mustard
1/2 teaspoon horseradish
Dash of hot sauce

Preheat oven to 450°F.

TO PREPARE SAUSAGE: Chop sausage into small pieces. In a nonstick or cast-iron skillet, heat canola oil; cook sausage until browned. Remove sausage from pan, drain on paper towels, and set aside.

Add onion and pepper to skillet and sauté until tender.

In a medium bowl, combine baking mix with milk. Mix in mustard, honey, sausage, onion, and pepper.

Form dough into teaspoon-sized balls and place on an ungreased cookie sheet. Sprinkle with garlic salt and bake for about 10 minutes until golden brown.

TO PREPARE SAUCE: Mix ingredients together in a small saucepan over medium-high heat. Serve turkey sausage bites and sauce warm.

Makes approximately 16 bites.
Serves 8.

ground poultry

Ground poultry—turkey or chicken—can be substituted for or combined with ground beef in most recipes. Be sure to ask for ground turkey or chicken **breast** to reduce the fat.

APPROXIMATE PER SERVING: *120 calories; 5 grams of fat*

Hot Spiced Cider

2 lemons
2 oranges
7 cups apple cider
5 cups cranberry juice cocktail
4 3-inch cinnamon sticks
2 teaspoons whole allspice
10 whole cloves
2-1/4-inch pieces fresh ginger, peeled and thinly sliced

Using a citrus zester or sharp vegetable peeler, carefully remove the rind from the lemons and oranges. Avoid peeling the white flesh beneath the rind.

Slice the citrus rind into 1/4-inch-thick strips.

Combine the rind, cider, cranberry juice, and spices in a large saucepan or Dutch oven. Over medium heat, bring the mixture to a simmer.

Reduce liquid for 30 minutes.

Strain cider, discarding the solids. Serve warm.

Makes approximately 8 cups.
Serves 8.

cinnamon or cassia?

Most ground cinnamon is really cassia (which is a member of the same family as true cinnamon but has a stronger flavor) or a combination of cinnamon and cassia. Both cinnamon and cassia are harvested from the bark of a plant in the laurel family. The outer layer of the bark is removed, and the inner bark curls up as it dries.

APPROXIMATE PER SERVING: *196 calories; 0.2 grams of fat*

Herb-Rubbed Pork Loin with Apricot-Pecan Stuffing

You can substitute kitchen twine with plain unwaxed dental floss.

Stuffing:

1 teaspoon canola oil
2 medium onions, diced finely
1 cup dried apricots, diced finely
2 stalks celery, diced finely
3 tablespoons pecans, finely chopped
1 teaspoon poultry seasoning
1 teaspoon garlic salt
1 cup brown rice, cooked in chicken broth

Pork:

4 pounds whole lean pork loin or 2 2-pound whole lean pork loins
1/3 cup dried thyme leaves
1/2 teaspoon garlic salt

Glaze:

1/2 cup apricot preserves
3 tablespoons corn syrup

TO PREPARE STUFFING: Heat oil in a nonstick skillet on medium-high heat and sauté onions until tender. Add apricots, celery, and pecans and cook 2 to 3 minutes.

Mix in poultry seasoning, garlic salt, and prepared rice.

Set aside.

(continued on next page)

a word on cooking pork

Check for an internal temperature from 150°F to 165°F when cooking pork. This will not only ensure thoroughly cooked pork, it will also produce a juicy, tender product. Many cookbooks recommend a temperature from 170°to 185°F, which can produce overcooked meat.

TO PREPARE PORK LOIN: Preheat oven to 375°F.

Trim all fat from pork. Cut down center to form cavity for stuffing. (If using 2 pork loins, split each).

Fill loin with stuffing mixture and tie together with kitchen twine.

Rub loin with thyme and garlic salt.

Bake approximately 30 minutes (or until no longer pink inside). After pork loin has been removed from the oven, cool for 5 minutes before slicing into 16 pieces.

TO PREPARE GLAZE: Bring apricot preserves and corn syrup to a boil over medium-high heat in a small saucepan.

Pour glaze over pork loin.

Serves 8.

APPROXIMATE PER SERVING: *489 calories; 17 grams of fat*

Spinach Soufflé

1 medium onion, finely chopped
6 cups fresh spinach, cleaned, dried, and chopped
1/4 teaspoon salt
1/4 teaspoon nutmeg
1/2 cup reduced-fat baking mix
1 cup skim or 1% milk
2 eggs
2 tablespoon Parmesan cheese, grated
Cooking spray

Preheat oven to 375°F.

Heat a medium skillet over medium-high heat and lightly coat with cooking spray. Sauté onion until tender. Add spinach and cook until wilted; drain if necessary. Season onion and spinach mixture with salt and nutmeg.

Spread spinach mixture in an 8 × 8-inch pan coated with cooking spray.

Mix together baking mix, milk, and eggs in a small bowl and pour over spinach and onion mixture.

Sprinkle with Parmesan cheese and bake for 30 minutes until lightly browned and firm.

Cool slightly and cut into small squares.

Serves 8.

APPROXIMATE PER SERVING: *80 calories; 3 grams of fat*

Harvest Rice

1 tablespoon margarine
1-1/3 cups carrots, thinly sliced
2-1/3 cups water
1 cup apple juice
3 tablespoons fresh lemon juice
3 tablespoons light brown sugar
1 teaspoon salt (optional)
1-1/2 cups rice
3/4 cup raisins
1/2 teaspoon cinnamon
3 cups apples, skin on, sliced
3/4 cup green onions, sliced
1 tablespoon sesame seeds

Melt margarine in a large skillet over low heat. Add carrots and sauté for 5 minutes or until tender-crisp.

Add water, apple and lemon juice, brown sugar, and salt. Mix well. Bring to a boil over medium heat. Stir in rice, raisins, and cinnamon. Cover, reduce heat, and simmer for 15 minutes or until rice is tender. Stir in apples and green onions and cook until heated through.

Meanwhile, toast sesame seeds in a preheated nonstick cooking pan. Brown over medium heat until golden. Remove from heat and allow to cool.

Spoon rice mixture into a serving dish.

Sprinkle toasted sesame seeds over top.

Serves 8.

APPROXIMATE PER SERVING: *246 calories; 3 grams of fat*

Pumpkin Mousse

Prepare this alternative to pumpkin pie ahead of time and keep chilled until ready to serve.

2 15-ounce cans unsweetened pumpkin
2 5.1-ounce packages vanilla instant pudding mix
2 tablespoons plus 1 teaspoon cinnamon, divided
1 teaspoon allspice
1 teaspoon nutmeg
5 cups fat-free whipped topping
17 graham cracker squares, broken into small pieces

In a large mixing bowl, stir together pumpkin, pudding mix, 2 tablespoons of cinnamon, and allspice and nutmeg. Fold in 4 cups of whipped topping until well blended.

To assemble, place graham cracker pieces in a large glass trifle bowl.

Top crackers with pumpkin mixture. Top pumpkin mixture with remaining whipped topping.

Sprinkle with remaining cinnamon.

Chill at least 3 hours before serving.

Serves 8.

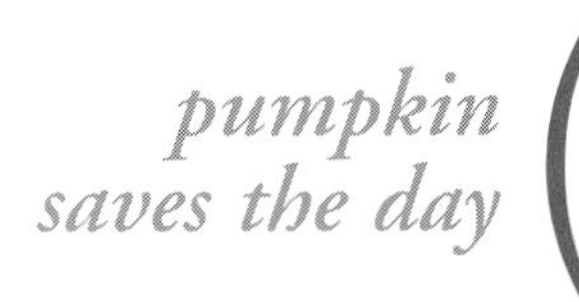

History books proclaim the pumpkin a hero! This awkward-looking fruit helped prevent starvation among the pilgrims during their first winter in America.

APPROXIMATE PER SERVING: *150 calories; 2 grams of fat*

NOTES

Game Night

Game Night is a great way to spend time with family and friends—and you'll actually be able to talk and enjoy each other instead of watching TV or a movie.

Prepare these recipes any time of the year for a card group that meets regularly or for a one-time game event. If you plan on more than 8 players, recipes can easily be doubled.

You may also want to place healthy munchies in small dishes on playing tables; party mix, raisins or dried fruit, popcorn, and pretzels should crave players' hunger in between courses.

menu for 8

- Three Bean Creole Dip
- Game Piece Grapes
- Flip Juice
- "Full" House Salad
- Turkey Reuben Grilled Sandwiches
- Eggplant Pizza
- Scrumptious Carrot Cake

Invitations

- Glue card stock printed with event information to an actual playing card or include the playing card in a handwritten, folded invitation.

Decorations

- Decorate with a red and black color scheme to coordinate with playing card colors. Using sponges and fabric paint, hand-stamp white tablecloths with red and black hearts, clubs, spades, and diamonds.

- Arrange red and white flowers in a black vase. Use red and black paper plates and napkins in keeping with the theme and for easy cleanup.

- If you'll have a large number of guests, set up card tables.

Activities

- Set up card or board games. Depending on the game and the number of guests, players can be split into groups of 4 or 6. You may need to provide paper and pencils for scorekeeping.

- Card game possibilities: bunco, pinochle, hearts, bridge, or brand-name games such as Uno, Go Fish, and Skip-Bo.

- Other game possibilities: backgammon, checkers, cribbage, or brand-name games such as Monopoly, Life, Trivial Pursuit, and Pictionary.

Setting the Scene

- Play soft jazz or contemporary music in the background so as not to interfere with play. Here are some possibilities we came up with, but play whatever suits your crowd:
  Fingerbreaker—Classics of Ragtime and Early Jazz by various artists
  A Morning in the Australian Bush by Andrew Skeoch and Sarah Koschak
  The Mirror Pool by Lisa Gerrard
  Paint the Sky with Stars: The Best of Enya by Enya
  Eden by Sarah Brightman

Three Bean Creole Dip

Serve with chopped fresh veggies, elegantly called crudités. Offer hot pepper sauce on the side.

1 15-ounce can kidney beans, drained
1 15-ounce can black beans, drained
1 15-ounce can Great Northern white beans, drained
1-1/2 teaspoons Creole (or Cajun) seasoning
1/4 red onion, diced
1 tomato, diced
1/2 green pepper, cored, seeded, and diced

Place half of each type of bean in a food processor. Add Creole seasoning and process until smooth.

Transfer processed beans to a medium serving bowl and stir in whole beans.

Top dip with onion, tomato, and green pepper.

Serve with assorted raw vegetables and hot pepper sauce.

Serves 8.

creole versus cajun

Many people believe Creole and Cajun methods of cooking are the same. While there are many similarities, Creole cooking uses more tomatoes and Cajun uses more spices.

APPROXIMATE PER SERVING: *166 calories; 1 gram of fat*

Game Piece Grapes

Flame or Ruby red seedless grapes are good varieties to use in this recipe.

32 red grapes, washed and dried
1/3 cup chive and onion light or fat-free cream cheese
2/3 cup almonds, chopped finely
2/3 cup fresh chives, chopped finely

Coat each grape with approximately 1/2 teaspoon of cream cheese. Roll each in almonds and chives.

Serve on toothpicks.

Chill until serving.

Makes approximately 32 grapes.
Serves 8.

grapes

The pale gray film found on some grapes is bloom, a natural waterproofing protection produced by grapes.

APPROXIMATE PER SERVING: *88 calories; 6 grams of fat*

Flip Juice

4 cups pineapple juice
4 cups cranberry juice cocktail
1 cup fresh lime juice
2 11-1/2-ounce cans apricot nectar
2 limes, cut into slices
4 12-ounce cans ginger ale

In a large pitcher, blend the first 5 ingredients. Cover and chill.

Add ginger ale just before serving, and mix thoroughly.

Serve over ice.

Makes approximately 20 cups.
Serves 8.

nectar or juice?

Nectar is thicker than juice because it contains fruit pulp. Some nectars are so thick that water is added during processing to make the juice more drinkable.

APPROXIMATE PER SERVING: *228 calories; 0.2 grams of fat*

"Full" House Salad

Make this tabbouleh salad the day before, as it requires overnight refrigeration.

1 cup uncooked bulghur or cracked wheat
2 cups boiling water
1/2 teaspoon salt
1/4 cup rice vinegar
2 tablespoons water
2 teaspoons extra-virgin olive oil
1/2 teaspoon salt
1/2 teaspoon coarsely ground black pepper
3/4 cup crumbled feta cheese with basil and tomato (approximately 3 ounces)
1/3 cup dried currants or raisins
1/4 cup minced green onions
1/4 cup minced fresh mint
1 tablespoon chopped fresh (or 1 teaspoon dried) basil
1 teaspoon grated lemon rind
12 cherry tomatoes, quartered
2 garlic cloves, minced

Combine bulghur or cracked wheat, boiling water, and salt in a large bowl. Cover and set aside for 30 minutes.

Meanwhile, combine vinegar, water, oil, salt, and pepper in a small bowl. Whisk dressing thoroughly.

Add feta cheese and the remaining ingredients to bulghur. Pour dressing over the bulghur mixture in the large bowl. Toss to mix well.

Cover and refrigerate overnight or for at least 8 hours.

Makes approximately 4 cups.
Serves 8.

According to folklore, the armies of Genghis Khan regarded bulghur, a partially cooked cracked wheat product, as one of their favorite foods.

APPROXIMATE PER SERVING: *98 calories; 3.1 grams of fat*

Turkey Reuben Grilled Sandwiches

4 tablespoons fat-free Thousand Island salad dressing, divided
8 slices dark pumpernickel bread
8 1/2-ounce slices light Swiss cheese
8 ounces turkey breast
3/4 cup sauerkraut
1 teaspoon caraway seeds
Butter-flavored cooking spray

Spread dressing on one side of each slice of bread.

Top 4 slices of bread with one slice of cheese each.

Top cheese with turkey breast, sauerkraut, caraway seeds, and second piece of cheese. Cover with second piece of bread.

Heat a nonstick skillet to medium-high; lightly coat with cooking spray.

Place sandwich in pan. Cook 1 minute. Spray top side of sandwich, flip, and cook an additional minute until crispy and cheese is melted.

Cool slightly and cut in half.

Makes 4 full sandwiches.
Serves 8.

what's in a name?

Arthur Reuben is credited with creating the first Reuben sandwich in 1914 for film star Annette Seelos. Omaha grocer Reuben Kay made a version of it for his poker buddies, but the sandwich gained prominence when one of his poker buddies' employees submitted the recipe for a sandwich contest in 1955 and won.

APPROXIMATE PER SERVING: *117 calories; 2 grams of fat*

Eggplant Pizza

To avoid the sometimes bitter taste of eggplant, salt both sides of the slices, let stand for 30 minutes, then rinse well in cool water. Pat the slices dry and use according to recipe.

1/2 package frozen bread dough, thawed
1/4 teaspoon olive oil
1 medium eggplant, sliced crosswise into 1/2-inch slices and grilled until browned
8 Roma tomatoes, sliced crosswise into 1/2 inch slices
1/2 cup artichoke hearts
1 tablespoon black olives, chopped
1/4 teaspoon garlic salt
2 tablespoons basil, fresh, chopped
1 tablespoon Parmesan cheese
1/3 cup mozzarella cheese

Preheat oven to 350°F.

Press bread dough onto a pizza pan or cookie sheet, forming crust. Rub dough lightly with olive oil. Top crust with eggplant, tomatoes, artichoke hearts, and olives.

Sprinkle with garlic salt, basil, Parmesan, and mozzarella cheese.

Bake 15 to 20 minutes on middle rack of oven until cheese is bubbling and crust is lightly browned.

Serves 8.

Did you know that eggplants are either male or female? Look at the rounded end—if the bottom is smooth, it's male; if it's indented, it's a female. Females have more seeds, which can taste bitter.

APPROXIMATE PER SERVING: *290 calories; 7 grams of fat*

Scrumptious Carrot Cake

To reward guests who stay to help you clean up, send them home with an extra slice of this yummy cake.

Cake:
1-1/3 cups sugar
1 cup natural applesauce (no sweetener added)
1/2 cup buttermilk
1 teaspoon vanilla
2 cups all-purpose flour
1 teaspoon baking powder
1 teaspoon baking soda
1 teaspoon salt
1 cup crushed pineapple, well drained
2 cups carrots, finely grated
1/2 cup walnuts, chopped and toasted
6 egg whites
Cooking spray

Frosting:
8 ounces low-fat cream cheese, softened
1 cup marshmallow crème
1 cup powdered sugar
1 teaspoon vanilla

Preheat oven to 350°F.

TO PREPARE THE CAKE: Combine sugar, applesauce, buttermilk, and vanilla in a medium bowl and mix well.

remove the fat

In many cake and cookie recipes, you can easily reduce the fat by substituting a portion of the oil or butter with applesauce. Keep in mind that any fat that's removed from a recipe needs to be replaced in whole or in part with other tenderizing ingredients like sugar or buttermilk, as it is in this theme's carrot cake recipe.

Sift together flour, baking powder, baking soda, and salt in a separate bowl. Slowly add to creamy mixture.

Add crushed pineapple, carrots, and walnuts, blending well.

In a mixing bowl, beat egg whites. Fold gently into batter.

Spray a 9 × 12-inch pan with vegetable cooking spray and spread batter evenly in pan.

Bake for 40 to 45 minutes. Cake is done when knife or toothpick, inserted in the center, comes out clean. Allow to cool 10 minutes before removing to cooling rack.

TO PREPARE THE FROSTING: Combine cream cheese, marshmallow crème, powdered sugar, and vanilla in a mixing bowl and blend well.

Place cake on serving platter. Spread frosting on cooled cake.

Serves 8.

APPROXIMATE PER SERVING: *218 calories; 5 grams of fat*

NOTES

Season's Greetings Holiday Affair

Host a small get-together so you can spend time with loved ones and also make your home festive for the holidays. A number of possible activities are perfect for children, such as making birdfeeders for outside trees or stringing popcorn and cranberries. Incorporate caroling into the evening's activities if it is part of your holiday traditions. Serve piping hot cocoa when the group returns.

menu for 8

- Spinach and Tomato Quesadilla Trees
- Hot Cocoa
- "Snow"-Dusted Fruit
- Hearty Veggie Alphabet Soup
- Confetti Beans and Rice
- Festive Tuna Rollups
- No-Bake Cookies

Invitations

- For relatively simple invitations, cut card stock in the shape of a tree, ornament, star, or any other holiday shape and write party information on it. Decorate with glitter or a stamped design if you wish.

Decorations

- Get the decorations started by making simple paper chains in holiday colors for banisters or doorframes or stringing white lights around doors.

- Serve food in baskets lined with either a glass or plastic dish and colored linen napkins. Use red and green, blue and white, red, black, and green, or any colors that reflect your holiday tradition.

- Display old-fashioned homespun decorations in muted country colors for a decorative and cozy touch. Include seasonal quilts, tin ornaments, raffia, or wooden, hand-painted ornaments.

Activities

- For craft activities, cover tables with brown packing paper and supply glue, seeds, pine cones, popcorn, cranberries, and string. Set up a craft area outside if appropriate or in an area that can easily be vacuumed.

- BIRD FEEDERS: Feed the birds in the middle of winter by making peanut butter–birdseed pinecones. Use cotton string for hanging and stringing so you avoid supplying children with sharp objects, such as ornament hangers or metal wire.

- GARLANDS: It's simple and fun to make strings of cranberries and popcorn. Place large jars of supplies such as cranberries and popcorn on the buffet table until ready to use so they double as decorations.

Take a Polaroid picture of the kids in front of their completed activity and give one to each child as a party favor. For a decorative touch, as the picture is developing, use a pencil to create a border or frame around the child.

- CAROLING: Spread some holiday cheer to friends, neighbors, a retirement community, or hospital by planning a caroling outing. Be sure to give your intended visitors some advance warning.

Setting the Scene

- Play festive music according to the traditions that you follow or sing your favorite holiday tunes, such as "Silent Night," "Rudolph the Red-Nosed Reindeer," or "Ma Oz Tsur" (traditionally sung after lighting the Hanukkah candles). You may want to play some classic videos in the background.

- Some music suggestions:
  Most Fabulous Classical Christmas Album Ever! by various traditional artists
  A Charlie Brown Christmas by the Vince Guaraldi Trio
  Long, Long Ago (A Jazz Celebration of Christmas, Chanukah & Kwanza) by Lynette Washington
  Kwanza by Archie Shepp

- Some Christmas video suggestions:
  It's a Wonderful Life, Miracle on 34th Street, Rudolph the Red-Nosed Reindeer, Frosty the Snowman, A Christmas Carol

- Video suggestions for children who celebrate Chanukah:
  Lamb Chop's Special Chanukah
  Lights: The Miracle of Chanukah
  There's No Such Thing as a Chanukah Bush, Sandy Goldstein

- Video suggestion for those who celebrate Kwanza:
  Celebration of Kwanza

Spinach and Tomato Quesadilla Trees

1 teaspoon canola oil
4 large whole-wheat tortillas
2/3 cup reduced-fat sharp cheddar cheese, shredded
1 cup spinach leaves, washed and dried
4 Roma tomatoes, sliced into thin slices
4 ounces of fat-free cream cheese
1/4 cup salsa

Heat oil in large nonstick or cast-iron skillet over medium-high heat.

Place one tortilla in skillet and top with 1/4 of the cheddar cheese. Add spinach and tomatoes.

Stir the cream cheese and salsa together. Spread half of it on the tomatoes.

Add another 1/4 of shredded cheese. Cover all with another tortilla. Cook 1 to 2 minutes.

Flip quesadilla over carefully. Cook another 1 to 2 minutes until crispy and cheese is melted.

Cool slightly and cut into 4 wedges. Prepare second quesadilla with remaining ingredients.

Makes 2 large quesaadillas.
Serves 8.

Fresh spinach is available year-round. Look for crisp, dark green leaves that have a fresh fragrance. Refrigerate for up to 3 days in a loose plastic bag.

APPROXIMATE PER SERVING: *170 calories; 4 grams of fat*

Hot Cocoa

6 ounces unsweetened baking chocolate
1 cup sugar
4 cups water
1/2 cup instant coffee
2 teaspoons ground cinnamon
1 teaspoon ground nutmeg
Dash of salt
8 cups skim or low-fat milk
Marshmallows as garnish (optional)

Combine all the ingredients except milk in saucepan or top of double boiler.

Heat over low heat, stirring constantly, until chocolate is melted and mixture is smooth.

Increase heat to boiling, then reduce heat. Cook uncovered, stirring constantly, for 4 minutes.

Stir in milk and heat until thoroughly hot.

Beat with hand mixer until foamy.

Garnish with marshmallows if desired and serve immediately.

Makes approximately 12 cups.
Serves 8.

marshmallows—an ancient treat

Marshmallows might be considered one of the world's oldest confections, dating back to ancient Egypt (2000 B.C.). Originating from the mallow plant, which grows wild in marshes, the root sap was beaten with sugar and egg whites. The result was a confection that was reserved for royalty.

APPROXIMATE PER SERVING: *250 calories; 4 grams of fat*

"Snow"-Dusted Fruit

1 cup orange slices, peeled and cubed
1 cup red grapes
1 cup green grapes
1 cup pineapple, cut into chunks
1 tablespoon pineapple juice
1 teaspoon honey
1/4 teaspoon lemon juice
1 tablespoon flaked and sweetened coconut

In a medium bowl, mix together orange, grapes, and pineapple.

In a small bowl, stir together pineapple juice, honey, and lemon juice. Toss fruit with juice mixture and transfer to serving dish.

Sprinkle fruit with coconut and chill before serving.

Makes approximately 4 cups.
Serves 8.

the multipurpose coconut

Every part of the coconut palm (the plant that produces coconuts) can be used, whether processed or in its natural form. The coconut meat is edible, coconut juice is a drink, the shells can serve as bowls, the fiber becomes nets, the leaves can be woven into baskets, the wood is used for building, and the roots can become fuel.

APPROXIMATE PER SERVING: *49 calories; 1 gram of fat*

Hearty Veggie Alphabet Soup

1 teaspoon olive oil
1 large onion, diced
8 cups vegetable broth
2 large carrots, cut into thin coins
1 15-ounce can corn, drained
1 stalk celery, diced
4 ounces mushrooms, sliced
1 cup alphabet pasta, uncooked
1 teaspoon oregano

In a large stockpot over medium-high heat, sauté onion in olive oil until tender. Add vegetable broth, carrots, corn, celery, and mushrooms and bring to a boil.

Add pasta and oregano and reduce heat.

Simmer for 15 minutes.

Makes approximately 8 cups.
Serves 8.

serving size

If soup is not intended as the main course, as it is in this theme, you can estimate that one quart (or 4 cups) serves four to six. As a main dish, however, plan on two servings per quart.

APPROXIMATE PER SERVING: *108 calories; 3 grams of fat*

Confetti Beans and Rice

One cup of uncooked long-grain white rice yields approximately 3 to 4 cups of cooked rice.

4 cups cooked long-grain rice
1 cup chopped plum tomato
1 4-1/2-ounce can chopped green chiles, drained
1 15-ounce can black beans, drained
1 10 ounce package frozen whole-kernel corn, thawed
1/3 cup chopped green onions
2 tablespoons chopped fresh cilantro

Cook rice according to package directions.

Stir in the remaining ingredients and cook until thoroughly heated, stirring frequently.

Makes approximately 8 cups.
Serves 8.

spilling the beans

Beans are rich in protein, fiber, phosphorus, and iron. They're easily grown or stored (dry or canned), and beans are essential throughout the world where animal protein is too expensive or unavailable.

APPROXIMATE PER SERVING: *203 calories; 2 grams of fat*

Festive Tuna Roll-Ups

Tuna packed in water contains far fewer calories, cholesterol, and fat than tuna packed in oil.

1 6-ounce can white tuna in water, drained and flaked
1 tablespoon light mayonnaise
4 tortillas, spinach (green), tomato (red), or whole-wheat
8 dill pickle spears
4 carrots, shredded
8 pepper rings, green or red

Mix tuna and mayonnaise in a small bowl.

Lay out each tortilla. Spread tuna in a line down the center of each. Top tuna with 2 pickles per tortilla and carrots.

Roll each tortilla burrito-style; keep closed by wrapping 2 pepper rings around each tortilla.

Cut each rollup in half and center pepper ring on each half.

Serves 8.

tuna tips

Always wipe the blade(s) of a can opener after using it on tuna or any other canned item.

APPROXIMATE PER SERVING: *190 calories; 3 grams of fat*

No-Bake Cookies

1/2 cup reduced-fat smooth peanut butter
1/2 cup honey
1/2 cup low-fat granola
1/2 cup crispy rice cereal
1/2 cup raisins
1/2 cup crushed graham crackers

Heat peanut butter and honey in a saucepan over low heat until creamy.

Remove from heat and pour into a bowl to cool.

Add granola, cereal, raisins, and crushed graham crackers to the peanut butter mix and stir well.

Roll into tablespoon-sized balls and set on wax paper.

Refrigerate at least 1 hour before serving.

Makes approximately 32 cookies.
Serves 8.

granola grievances

In recent years, granola has gotten a bad rap for being a high-fat, high-calorie "health" food. Although granola and muesli are excellent sources of fiber, the main nutritional information to evaluate is sugar, calories, and fat grams. Most commercial granolas are toasted and sweetened, which means added fat, sugar, and calories. The healthiest products contain 5 grams of sugar and 150 calories per serving or less.

APPROXIMATE PER SERVING: *155 calories; 5 grams of fat*

NOTES

NOTES

Post-Holiday Blues Party

This fun theme is a great way to overcome the letdown at the end of holiday season. Get friends together for a party designed to cheer up everyone, add some food and fun, and see how fun January can be!

menu for 8

- Green Chile Artichoke Dip
- Blue Storm
- Mixed Greens with Berry-Mustard Vinaigrette
- "I Got the Blues" Chicken
- Couscous with Almonds, Dried Blueberries, and Parmesan Cheese
- Roasted Garlicky Potatoes
- Lemon Cake with Brandied Blueberry Sauce

Decorations

- Keep "blue" in mind when you're decorating: use a blue tablecloth, blue napkins, and blue and white serving dishes, plates, and cups. Use blue light bulbs in certain light fixtures, such as the bathroom, entry or foyer, serving area, or outside front light.

- Check with a local florist on the availability of blue and white flowers. Place them in a black vase.

- As host, you may choose to wear a completely blue outfit.

Invitations

- Cut dark blue card stock into 4 × 4-inch squares. Paste a 3 × 3-inch piece of thick white paper with party information onto the card stock. Request that guests wear blue or black.

- SAMPLE WORDING: We're all mourning the end of another holiday season…We all miss the food, family, and festivities…Who needs a better excuse for a Post-Holiday Blues Party? Wear blue or black, but come prepared for fun!

Activities

- Hold a blues music lip sync contest. Give prizes guaranteed to cheer up guests, such as tickets to a comedy club or a massage.

Setting the Scene

- The music for this theme should be none other than the Blues.

- For the lip sync contest, try to obtain the words for a couple of the songs.

- Some music suggestions:
  Windy City Blues by Muddy Waters
  The Blues Brothers: Original Soundtrack Recording by the Blues Brothers
  Essential Southern Rock produced by the House of Blues and performed by various artists
  Blues Traveler by Blues Traveler
  The Best of the Moody Blues by the Moody Blues

- You can also play some of the Blues Brothers movies in the background during the party:
  The Blues Brothers
  Best of the Blues Brothers
  Blues Brothers 2000

Green Chile Artichoke Dip

Serve this dip with blue corn chips.

2 14-ounce cans artichoke hearts, packed in water, drained well
3 tablespoons plus 2 tablespoons grated Parmesan cheese, divided
1/4 cup light mayonnaise
2 4-ounce cans green chiles, chopped
1 15-ounce can Great Northern beans, drained well
3 teaspoons paprika
Dash of jalapeño pepper sauce, or to taste
3 teaspoons garlic salt

Preheat oven to 350°F.

Chop artichoke hearts into bite-sized pieces.

In a medium bowl, mix artichoke hearts and remaining ingredients, reserving 2 tablespoons of Parmesan cheese. Spread mixture into a 8 × 8-inch baking pan. Top with remaining Parmesan cheese.

Bake for 20 minutes until bubbling and slightly browned.

Serve immediately.

Serves 8.

Blue corn, which appears black on the stalk, is a type of corn that turns blue as the kernels dry. It is ground into cornmeal and used to make tortillas and chips, just like yellow corn. If you don't see bags of blue corn chips in the normal snack aisle, look in the natural food sections of supermarkets. Don't be surprised if you also see red!

APPROXIMATE PER SERVING: *162 calories; 3 grams of fat*

Blue Storm

2 cups fresh orange juice
3/4 cup papaya or mango nectar
1 cup pineapple juice
1/4 cup blue daiquiri mix
Dash of blue vegetable coloring
Freshly grated nutmeg as garnish

Combine orange, papaya or mango, and pineapple juices in a large pitcher. Chill.

Place blue daiquiri mix in a small pitcher. Add blue vegetable coloring until desired color has been achieved.

Fill glasses with ice cubes. Pour 1/4 cup of orange juice mixture into each glass.

Slowly pour 1 tablespoon of blue liquid down the inside of each glass. Do not stir before serving. Garnish with nutmeg if desired.

Makes approximately 4 cups.
Serves 8.

floral ice cubes

For a decorative touch to your ice cubes, place an edible flower in each ice cube tray section. Fill with water and freeze.

APPROXIMATE PER SERVING: *84 calories; 0 grams of fat*

Mixed Greens with Berry-Mustard Vinaigrette

8 cups romaine and spinach, washed, dried, and torn
1/2 cup balsamic vinegar
2 tablespoons olive oil
3 tablespoons raspberry fruit spread
1-1/2 teaspoons Dijon mustard
1/4 teaspoon fresh tarragon, chopped
1 teaspoon garlic, minced
1 teaspoon chives
Dash of salt and pepper, to taste

Prepare salad greens and set aside.

Whisk remaining ingredients together in small bowl.

Chill and serve on mixed greens.

Makes 1 cup of dressing.
Serves 8.

facts about salad

Greens will wilt if left out to dry at room temperature. To revive them, rinse with cool water and dry in a salad spinner or on paper towels. Place the remainder in a roomy plastic bag and refrigerate.

APPROXIMATE PER SERVING: *62 calories; 3 grams of fat*

"I Got the Blues" Chicken

2 tablespoons olive oil
1/2 cup all-purpose flour
2 teaspoons garlic salt
8 boneless, skinless chicken breast halves
Cooking spray
2 teaspoons vegetable oil margarine
2 large onions, sliced lengthwise
6 cups mixed mushrooms, such as button, Portabella, or crimini
2 tablespoons lemon juice
2 cups fat-free chicken broth
2 cups seedless red grapes, halved
1/3 cup blue cheese, crumbled
Black pepper to taste

Heat olive oil in a large nonstick skillet over medium-high heat.

In a wide-mouthed dish, combine flour and garlic salt. Dip chicken breasts in flour mixture and place breast side down in skillet. Brown for 4 minutes.

Lightly coat chicken breasts with cooking spray and turn over, cooking 4 minutes on other side. Remove chicken from pan and set aside.

Add margarine and onions to pan and sauté for 1 minute. Add mushrooms and sauté for 3 additional minutes or until tender.

Add lemon juice; return chicken to pan.

Pour in chicken broth and simmer 5 minutes, making sure chicken is fully cooked.

Remove from heat, mix in grapes, and transfer to serving dish.

Sprinkle with blue cheese and black pepper.

Serves 8.

Blue cheese is cheese that has been treated with molds that make blue or green veins in the cheese and give it its characteristically strong flavor and smell, which intensify with aging.

APPROXIMATE PER SERVING: *62 calories; 3.5 grams of fat*

Couscous with Almonds, Dried Blueberries, and Parmesan Cheese

2-1/2 cups fat-free chicken broth
2 teaspoons garlic salt
2 cups couscous
2 tablespoons olive oil
1/2 cup dried blueberries
2 tablespoons slivered almonds
4 tablespoons grated or shredded Parmesan cheese, divided

In a medium saucepan, bring chicken broth and garlic salt to a boil.

Add couscous, stir, and remove from heat. Allow to sit for 5 minutes.

Mix in olive oil, blueberries, almonds, and 2 tablespoons of Parmesan cheese.

Transfer to serving dish and top with remaining 2 tablespoons of cheese.

Serves 8.

couscous considerations

Couscous is granular semolina, or durum wheat. It cooks very quickly and may be served as a side dish, part of a salad, or even sweetened and used in a dessert.

APPROXIMATE PER SERVING: *212 calories; 5 grams of fat*

Roasted Garlicky Potatoes

Blanching the potatoes and garlic before roasting cuts down on the cooking time.

2 heads of garlic
8 small blue potatoes, scrubbed and cubed
8 Yukon gold potatoes, scrubbed and cubed
8 fingerling potatoes, scrubbed and cubed
2 tablespoons chopped fresh rosemary
2 tablespoons olive oil
1/2 teaspoon salt and pepper, or to taste
Rosemary sprigs as garnish (optional)

Preheat oven to 425°F.

Without peeling or separating the cloves, remove the papery white outer skin from garlic heads.

Place garlic and potatoes in a large saucepan or Dutch oven. Cover with water and bring to a boil.

Meanwhile, combine the rosemary, oil, salt, and pepper in a large bowl.

Once the potatoes and garlic have come to a rolling boil, remove from heat, drain, and pat dry.

Mix the potatoes, garlic, and rosemary mixture together, tossing to coat. Arrange potatoes and garlic on a jelly-roll pan.

Bake for 30 minutes or until tender, shaking occasionally.

Separate the garlic head into cloves, discard skins, and serve with potatoes.

Garnish with rosemary sprigs, if desired.

Serves 8.

Many unusual new potatoes in the marketplace are actually heritage vegetables that date back centuries. All-blue potatoes are some of the most distinctive. These all-purpose potatoes are striking in color—from blue-purple to purple-black—and have a dense texture.

APPROXIMATE PER SERVING: *181 calories; 3.7 grams of fat*

Lemon Cake with Brandied Blueberry Sauce

Don't expect to have leftovers of this lemony dessert. The sauce is also delightful served over lemon yogurt.

Cake:

2 cups O-shaped cereal, finely ground in food processor
3/4 teaspoon salt
3/4 cup sugar
2 cups all-purpose flour
1/2 teaspoon baking soda
1/3 cup canola oil
1-3/4 cups buttermilk
2 eggs, beaten
1/4 cup fresh lemon juice
2 tablespoons lemon zest
2 tablespoons powdered sugar

Blueberry sauce:

1/2 cup plus 1 tablespoon brandy
2 tablespoons sugar
2 cups frozen blueberries
3 tablespoons lemon juice
1/2 teaspoon cornstarch
1 teaspoon cold water

Preheat oven to 400°F.

TO PREPARE CAKE: Grease and flour a 9-inch nonstick fluted tube pan.

In a medium mixing bowl, stir together cereal, salt, sugar, flour, and baking soda. Add oil, buttermilk, eggs, lemon juice, and lemon zest. Beat for 5 minutes on low speed until well blended.

Bake for 25 minutes until lightly browned. Cool cake completely.

Invert onto platter and sprinkle with powdered sugar.

TO PREPARE SAUCE: While cake is baking, heat brandy and sugar in a medium saucepan over medium-high heat, stirring constantly. Boil 3 minutes to reduce alcohol. Stir in 1 cup of blueberries and remove from heat.

Purée remaining cup of berries and lemon juice in food processor. Add purée to brandy mixture and return to a boil.

Mix cornstarch and water together in small cup. Add to saucepan, stirring until mixture thickens.

Cool slightly and serve over completely cooled lemon cake.

Makes 1-1/2 cups of sauce.
Serves 8.

the tasty blueberry

Blueberries are members of the genus Vaccinium and often grow wild, producing fruit in the summer months. They were named after the Latin word for cow, vacca, because cows love to eat them.

APPROXIMATE PER SERVING: *403 calories; 11 grams of fat*

NOTES

"Souper" Bowl Bash

Football fans live for Superbowl Sunday…and what better reason to invite friends over for a healthy meal featuring a variety of soups as the main menu items? Your guests don't have to enjoy football, just eating and fun.

menu for 8

- Kick-Off Crunch
- Spiced Ginger Tea
- Caesar Salad
- Sideline Chicken Chili
- Halfback Beef Burgundy Soup
- Touchdown Tomato-Basil Soup
- Fourth Quarter Chocolate Cheesecake

Invitations

- Cut football shapes from brown paper bags. Use a black marker to draw laces at the top of the footballs. Write party information in center of each.

- SAMPLE WORDING: Join us at the Gridiron for "Souper" Bowl Sunday festivities • Game clock is set for 7 PM, January 22 • Please arrive by 5 for food and fun •Wear your team's colors and dress for halftime activities!

Decorations

- Paint an inexpensive green tablecloth with white fabric paint to resemble the lines on a football field. Mark off thin lines with painter's tape and roll fabric paint between tape to make yard lines.

- Make numbers by using paint-dipped sponges cut into number shapes and pressing in appropriate places (for the 50-yard line, 40-yard line, and so on).

- Hang felt pennants from the ceiling and spread green Astroturf-style welcome mats on a coffee or buffet table. Serve appetizers and beverages on the "field" (it will also protect your furniture).

Activities

- GAME SHOW: Hold a Sports Trivia game show in which contestants work as teams to answer sports-related questions. As host and organizer, designate yourself to be the game show host, particularly if you create your own questions and multiple-choice answers. A commercially available sports trivia game or sports-related web site can supply you with questions.

- THE QUARTERBACK HALFTIME EVENT: Set up a football-related obstacle course in your backyard, basement, or spare room. Allow plenty of room to create a variety of contests. You may choose to organize teams or encourage individual competition. Some suggestions for "challenges" include:
- throwing a football through a makeshift goal
- putting on and taking off a giant football jersey (over the players' clothes) with one or both arms tied behind the back
- running through "tires," whether actual tires, those made with hula hoops, or imaginary ones drawn onto pavement or marked with tape on the basement floor will work.

- PICK-UP TOUCH FOOTBALL: Encourage your guests to form into two teams for a pick-up touch football game.

Setting the Scene

- Play the Superbowl on TV, but consider some of these music choices for the halftime events:
  We Are the Champions, We Will Rock You, Another One Bites the Dust by Queen
  Who Let the Dogs Out by Baha Men
  ESPN Presents: Jock Jams by various artists

Kick-Off Crunch

2 cups crispy corn cereal squares, such as Corn Chex
2 cups crispy wheat cereal squares, such as Wheat Chex
2 cups O-shaped cereal
2 cups pretzel twists
1/2 cup barbecue sauce
2 tablespoons canola oil
2 teaspoons brown sugar, packed
Dash of hot pepper sauce to taste

Preheat oven to 350°F.

Mix cereals and pretzels together in a large bowl.

In a medium saucepan, heat barbecue sauce, oil, sugar, and hot pepper sauce over medium-high heat until boiling, stirring constantly.

Pour sauce onto cereal mixture and stir until cereal is completely coated.

Spread mixture in a single layer on a baking sheet. Bake for 5 minutes, stir, and bake an additional 5 minutes.

Remove from oven and cool.

Makes approximately 8 cups.
Serves 8.

make a change

The cereals in this party mix are whole-grain foods. Research indicates that regular consumption of whole-grain foods in combination with a diet rich in fruits and vegetables and low in saturated fat may reduce the risk of certain cancers.

APPROXIMATE PER SERVING: *320 calories; 5 grams of fat*

Spiced Ginger Tea

Make this drink up to 6 hours in advance—simply chill until ready to use and reheat before serving. If you prefer strong tea, use an additional tea bag.

8 cups water
8 whole cardamom pods
6 fresh or crystallized ginger slices
4 1-1/2 × 3-inch orange peel strips (orange part only)
8 whole cloves
4 cups low-fat milk
2 tea bags of Darjeeling or Assam tea
1/3 cup packed dark brown sugar

In a large saucepan or Dutch oven, combine water, cardamom, ginger, orange peel strips, and cloves over medium-high heat. Cover, reduce heat, and simmer 10 minutes.

Add milk and tea bags. Bring to a boil for 2 minutes.

Remove from heat and allow the tea to steep for 4 to 6 minutes, or until desired strength is achieved. Strain to remove spices and fruit peel.

Stir in sugar.

Serve warm.

Makes approximately 12 cups.
Serves 8.

homemade crystallized ginger

Use the following simple directions to make your own crystallized ginger: • Peel 1 pound of fresh ginger root with a hand peeler. Slice very thinly. • Cover with water in a saucepan and cook gently until tender, about 30 minutes. Drain. • Weigh or estimate an equal amount of sugar. Replace ginger in the saucepan with sugar and 3 tablespoons of water. • Boil, stirring often, until the ginger is transparent and the liquid is almost evaporated. • Reduce heat to medium-low and cook until almost dry, continuing to stir constantly. • Toss the cooked ginger in plenty of sugar to coat. • Store in an airtight jar for up to three months.

APPROXIMATE PER SERVING: *80 calories; 0 grams of fat*

Caesar Salad

Make extra croutons for soup toppings if you desire.

Croutons and salad:
8 1-ounce slices French bread, cut into 3/4-inch cubes
16 cups torn Romaine lettuce, washed and dried

Dressing:
1/2 cup grated Parmesan cheese
1/2 cup fat-free mayonnaise
1/2 cup water
1/4 cup fresh lemon juice
1 teaspoon anchovy paste
1 teaspoon Worcestershire sauce
1/2 teaspoon freshly ground black pepper
1/4 teaspoon dry mustard
4 garlic cloves, minced

TO PREPARE CROUTONS: Preheat oven to 300°F. Spread bread cubes evenly on a cookie sheet.

Bake for 15 minutes or until lightly browned. Cool.

TO PREPARE DRESSING: While the croutons are baking, combine dressing ingredients and whisk until thoroughly blended.

TO PREPARE SALAD: Place lettuce in large bowl. Add croutons.

Add dressing and toss to coat.

Serve immediately.

Serves 8.

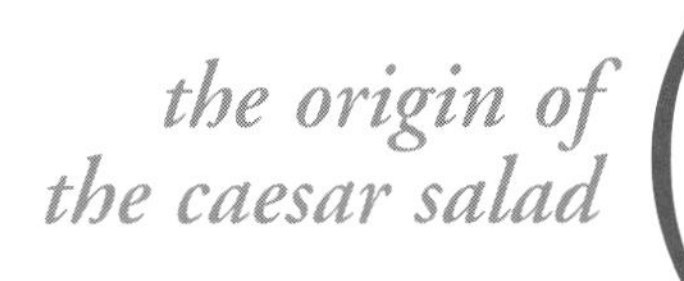

An Italian chef named Caesar Cardini, who owned a restaurant in Tijuana, Mexico, created the Caesar salad in 1924. It is said that the original dressing did not contain eggs or anchovies.

APPROXIMATE PER SERVING: *142 calories; 2.4 grams of fat*

Sideline Chicken Chili

3 skinless chicken breast halves, bone intact
6 cups water
1 large onion, sliced lengthwise
2 tablespoons cilantro
2 cups fat-free chicken broth
4 corn tortillas, cut into 1-inch strips
1 4-1/2-ounce can diced green chiles
1 15-ounce can corn, drained
2 15-ounce cans Great Northern beans (or other white bean)
1 cup green tomatoes or tomatillos, chopped into 1-inch pieces
1 tablespoon fajita seasoning
1/4 teaspoon garlic salt
1 tablespoon lime juice

Bring chicken, water, onion, and cilantro to a boil in a large stockpot. Reduce heat and simmer 20 minutes. Remove chicken and cool.

Meanwhile, in a small saucepan, bring chicken broth to a boil, stir in tortillas, and turn off heat.

Pull chicken off the bone and cut into bite-sized pieces. Return to stockpot. Add chiles, corn, beans, tomatoes, fajita seasoning, and garlic salt.

Add tortilla/broth mixture to stockpot and simmer 15 minutes.

Add lime juice to chili and serve.

Makes approximately 10 cups.
Serves 8.

a great leftover

Double or triple this recipe—chili freezes well. Serve it straight up or try one of these serving suggestions: fill a tortilla with chili, serve chili over spaghetti noodles, or top a baked potato with chili.

APPROXIMATE PER SERVING: *330 calories; 5 grams of fat*

Halfback Beef Burgundy Soup

2 teaspoons olive oil
1 large red onion, sliced lengthwise
1 large yellow onion, sliced lengthwise
6 cups fat-free beef broth
1-1/3 cups Burgundy wine
1-1/3 cups beet greens, tightly packed
1-1/2 pounds round steak, trimmed and cut into 1-inch cubes
1 teaspoon garlic salt
2 teaspoons thyme
2 small beets, cut into 1-inch cubes
1/2 cup quick-cooking barley

In a large stockpot, sauté onions in oil over medium-high heat until tender. Add broth, wine, and beet greens to pot. Bring to a boil, then reduce heat.

Season meat with garlic salt and thyme and add to pot.

Add beets and barley and simmer for 20 minutes.

Makes approximately 8 cups.
Serves 8.

advance preparation

Most savory soups and stews taste better if made a day or two in advance so the flavors have plenty of time to marry. Simply reheat before serving.

APPROXIMATE PER SERVING: *140 calories; 5 grams of fat*

Touchdown Tomato-Basil Soup

2 teaspoons olive oil
2 large onions, sliced lengthwise
4 cloves garlic, minced
2 cups chickpeas, drained
2 tablespoons fresh basil, chopped and divided
2 cups tomato sauce
4 cups fat-free vegetable broth
4 Roma tomatoes, diced
2 tablespoons grated Parmesan cheese

In a medium stockpot, sauté onions and garlic in oil over medium heat until tender.

Add chickpeas and 1 tablespoon of basil and sauté 1 minute. Add tomato sauce, broth, and tomatoes. Reduce heat and simmer for 15 minutes.

Stir in remaining basil a few minutes before serving.

Top with Parmesan cheese.

Makes approximately 8 cups.
Serves 8.

herb alert!

Keep in mind that herbs and seasonings have a more intense flavor if added at the end of the long cooking process.

APPROXIMATE PER SERVING: *130 calories; 3 grams of fat*

Fourth Quarter Chocolate Cheesecake

1 cup non-fat plain yogurt
4 ounces low-fat cream cheese
1/4 cup part-skim ricotta cheese
1/4 cup maple syrup
3 tablespoons cocoa powder
2 large egg whites
2 teaspoons ground cinnamon
1 teaspoon coffee liqueur or brewed coffee

Preheat oven to 350°F.

Coat an 8-inch pan with nonstick cooking spray. In blender purée yogurt, cream cheese, ricotta cheese, syrup, cocoa, egg whites, cinnamon, and coffee liqueur.

Pour into pan. Bake for 50 minutes or until set and cooked.

Let cool.

Serves 8.

ricotta reality

Ricotta is a cheese made from the whey drained off while making mozzarella or provolone. In Italian, the word ricotta translates to "recooked," because it's made from a by-product of another cheese.

APPROXIMATE PER SERVING: *98 calories; 4 grams of fat*

This Must Be Love Valentine's Day Dinner

Traditionally, Valentine's Day is a holiday that couples spend with only each other. Stir up this tradition by inviting friends over with their significant others. If you're part of a group of singles, get everyone together to share a delicious meal and meet each other. Who knows, maybe a match will be made!

This elegant but fun Valentine's dinner for couples highlights famous twosomes from the past and old-fashioned romance. Your friends will rave about the menu's red touches and will be grateful to avoid the lines at crowded restaurants.

menu for 8

- Polenta Hearts with Roasted Red Pepper and Olive Tapenade
- Valentine Spritzers
- Fruits of Love Salad with Blushed Vinaigrette
- Rosemary Beef with Shallot Sauce
- Buttermilk Garlic Mashed Potatoes
- Ruby Red Beets with Fennel
- Made in Heaven Strawberry Mousse

Invitations

- Set up the evening's theme with an invitation featuring a black-and-white photocopy or old-fashioned sepia-toned picture of a famous couple, a romantic scene, or a famous kiss. Write or print party information on the back. If your guests are game, ask that they come dressed as their favorite famous couple or as romantic figures from the past.

- Or send simple invitations—commercially printed old-fashioned Valentine's Day cards.

- You can make easy homemade Valentine's invitations using red tissue and paper lace doilies. These old-fashioned paper doilies are easy to find in February.

Decorations

- Red has always been regarded as the color of love and passion; set it off with rich tones of gold. Add special touches by arranging red or gold balloons, candles, or little trinkets to the scene.

- Set the table with a red tablecloth and napkins tied with gold cords. Group multiple candles on the table, in the bathroom, in the foyer, and other places around the house to create a dramatic effect. Consider using a rose-colored light bulb in the entryway or foyer.

- Offer your best china, or for a big-screen influenced style, use inexpensive gold plates and serving pieces or even gold chargers and gold-edged glassware to evoke the golden age of Hollywood.

- Place a variety of pink, rose, and red roses or flowers in a large glass vase as a centerpiece or in smaller vases around the house.

Activities

- Before guests arrive, write the name of a person who has shared a role within a famous on-screen or off-screen couple on a 3 × 5 card. (Some examples are Romeo or Juliet, Spencer Tracy or Katherine Hepburn, the Duke of York or Wallace Simpson, Rhett Butler or Scarlett O'Hara, and so on.) When guests arrive, tape a card to each person's back. Guests may ask each other only yes or no questions to determine the identity of the person on their card.

- Arrange place cards on the table of the other half of the couple on their 3 × 5 card. After they have identified the person on their card, inform guests that they should sit at their "other half's" name.

- For after-dinner entertainment, consider hiring a dance instructor or having an instruction tape for waltzes, the tango, or country line dancing.

Setting the Scene

- You can probably find an endless selection of romantic music and videos to play in the background. We took the opportunity of providing you with some classic possibilities:

  Music:
  My Funny Valentine by Chet Baker
  Songs for Swinging Lovers by Frank Sinatra
  The Greatest Hits by Nat King Cole
  Heart Shaped World by Chris Isaak
  Faith by Faith Hill
  We Are In Love by Harry Connick Jr.

  Video:
  Gone with the Wind / Casablanca / From Here to Eternity
  The Philadelphia Story / When Harry Met Sally...

Polenta Hearts with Roasted Red Pepper and Olive Tapenade

Make the polenta the day before to save time. Get your heart-shaped cookie cutter ready so you can make the polenta hearts.

Polenta:
4 cups water
Dash of salt
1-1/3 cups yellow cornmeal
1-1/3 cups cold water
Cooking spray

Tapenade:
2 tablespoons roasted red peppers in vinegar, drained and chopped
3 Roma tomatoes, diced finely
3 tablespoons Kalamata or other black olives, chopped finely
2 tablespoons barley, cooked
2 tablespoons parsley, chopped finely

2 tablespoons Feta cheese, crumbled

quick polenta recipe

Polenta is cornmeal cooked with milk or water. It can be soft and porridge-like or cooled, cut into pieces, and fried. This creamy polenta recipe can serve 8 as a simple side dish: 8 cups of water, 2 teaspoons of salt, 2 cups of coarse cornmeal, Parmesan and fresh herbs, such as thyme, sage, or rosemary. Bring 8 cups of water and salt to boil in a heavy large saucepan. Add cornmeal and whisk until combined. Reduce heat to low, cover, and simmer until polenta is thick and pulls away from the side of the pan, stirring frequently, 30 to 40 minutes.

APPROXIMATE PER SERVING: *90 calories; 1.5 grams of fat*

TO PREPARE POLENTA: Bring 4 cups of water and salt to a boil in a medium saucepan.

Meanwhile, mix cornmeal with cold water. Add to the boiling water. Cook over medium heat for 25 minutes, stirring constantly.

Line an 8 × 8-inch baking pan with plastic wrap. Coat lightly with cooking spray. Pour cooked cornmeal into baking pan.

Chill at least 3 hours.

Cut into heart shapes with a medium heart-shaped cookie cutter. Place polenta hearts on a baking sheet that has been lightly coated with cooking spray.

Set oven to broil.

Broil polenta until barely browned. Turn over and broil the other side. Remove from oven and set aside.

TO PREPARE TAPENADE: In a small bowl, mix together remaining ingredients except cheese.

Top each heart with tapenade and sprinkle with cheese.

Makes approximately 24 hearts.
Serves 8.

APPROXIMATE PER SERVING: *90 calories; 1.5 grams of fat*

Valentine Spritzers

Chill the soda first—carbonated drinks remain fizzy longer if they've been chilled before opening.

1 64-ounce bottle cranberry-raspberry juice
2 tablespoons grenadine
1 liter lemon-lime soda, chilled
2 cups club soda, chilled
Maraschino cherries for garnish

Combine juice and grenadine and mix well.

Add sodas just before serving. Add a maraschino cherry to each glass as a garnish.

Makes approximately 14-1/2 cups.
Serves 8.

cool cubes

Make ice cubes out of the types of juice you're serving so that they don't dilute the drink as they melt.

APPROXIMATE PER SERVING: *220 calories; 0 grams of fat*

Fruits of Love Salad with Blushed Vinaigrette

To cut the amount of fat in this salad, begin by adding only 1/3 cup of olive oil to the dressing mix. Increase the amount in small increments until the balance of flavors tastes right to you.

Salad:

4 cups mixed salad greens, washed, dried, and torn
4 cups spinach, washed, dried, and torn
1-1/2 cups fresh strawberries, hulled and sliced thinly
1 cup pink grapefruit, cut into pieces
1/2 red onion, thinly sliced

Vinaigrette:

1/4 cup red onion, minced
2/3 cup olive oil
1/4 cup red wine vinegar
1 tablespoon balsamic vinegar
2 teaspoons Dijon mustard

Combine salad ingredients in a large bowl and toss well. Refrigerate until ready to serve.

TO PREPARE VINAIGRETTE: Combine ingredients in a jar. Cover tightly. Shake well. Pour vinaigrette over salad and gently toss to coat.

Makes 1 cup of dressing.
Serves 8.

vinegar: sour grapes

Vinegar is a sour condiment made by fermenting wine, beer, or cider. Balsamic vinegar is made from white Trebbiano grapes. It gets its dark color and sweet, pungent flavor from the barrels in which it is aged a minimum of twelve years. Use sparingly so its intense flavor does not overwhelm.

APPROXIMATE PER SERVING: *190 calories; 9 grams of fat*

Rosemary Beef with Shallot Sauce

Serve this skillet dish over rice if you wish.

2 pounds lean round steak, thinly sliced and cut into bite-sized pieces
1/2 teaspoon black pepper
2 teaspoons fresh rosemary, chopped
1/2 teaspoon garlic salt
2 teaspoons olive oil
4 shallots, finely chopped
1 medium sweet red pepper, chopped
1 pound mushrooms, sliced
1/2 cup light sour cream
1/4 cup light cream cheese
Rosemary sprigs for garnish

Season steak pieces with pepper, rosemary, and garlic salt.

Heat olive oil in a large skillet over medium-high heat. Add shallots and red pepper; sauté until tender, about 2 minutes.

Add steak and sauté 2 to 3 minutes or until slightly browned. Add mushrooms and cook until tender.

Remove from heat and mix in sour cream and cream cheese.

Garnish with fresh rosemary sprigs, if desired.

Serves 8.

shallot sense

Shallots are bulbs covered with papery skin like garlic cloves. Their cream-colored flesh is usually slightly tinged with green or purple. Shallots taste like mild onions and can be used whenever onions are called for.

APPROXIMATE PER SERVING: *210 calories; 7 grams of fat*

Buttermilk Garlic Mashed Potatoes

12 medium red potatoes, scrubbed and quartered, skin on
6 cloves garlic, peeled
1 teaspoon salt for water
Water to cover
1/2 teaspoon olive oil
1 teaspoon salt for seasoning
Pepper to taste
1 cup buttermilk
3 scallions, chopped finely

In a medium saucepan, mix potatoes, garlic, and 1 teaspoon of salt. Add enough water to cover and bring to a boil. Boil 20 minutes until potatoes are tender. Drain.

Return potatoes and garlic to saucepan; add oil, salt, pepper, and buttermilk. Warm over medium heat until hot but not boiling.

Remove from heat and mash with potato masher or electric beater until fluffy.

Transfer to heated serving dish and sprinkle with scallions.

Makes approximately 12 cups.
Serves 8.

wash your hands of garlic

Specialty stores sell metal tools meant to rid your hands of garlic odor, but you can achieve the same effect with simple stainless steel measuring spoons. After peeling and chopping garlic, rub the rounded side of a stainless steel measuring spoon against your fingers under running water. Then wash with soap and water. (Try chewing fresh parsley to help get rid of your garlicky breath—especially on Valentine's Day! It will help diminish the garlic smell.)

APPROXIMATE PER SERVING: *90 calories; 2 grams of fat*

Ruby Red Beets with Fennel

4 large beets, peeled and cut into 3/4-inch-thick heart shapes
1-1/2 cups fennel root, sliced (or 1-1/2 cups celery plus 1 tablespoon fennel seed)
2 tablespoons sugar
4 tablespoons balsamic vinegar, divided
1 teaspoon olive oil

Preheat oven to 350°F.

Place beets and fennel in a baking dish. Sprinkle with sugar, 1 tablespoon of balsamic vinegar, and olive oil. Stir until coated.

Bake for 1 hour until beets are tender.

Splash with remaining vinegar and serve.

Serves 8.

fennel facts

Fennel is part of the carrot family. In U.S. markets you'll mainly find the fennel bulb, which resembles an onion. Fennel bulbs are mild in flavor and are versatile enough to be braised, cooked in soups, or sliced and mixed into a salad raw. If you have the feathery fennel foliage, snip the fronds and add them to your dish as well.

APPROXIMATE PER SERVING: *45 calories; 0.7 grams of fat*

Made in Heaven Strawberry Mousse

3 cups quartered strawberries
1/4 cup sugar
3/4 cup low-fat sour cream
2 cups frozen reduced-calorie whipped topping

In a blender or food processor, combine strawberries and sugar. Process until smooth. Pour contents into a large bowl. Add sour cream and mix well using a whisk. Fold whipped topping into strawberry mixture.

Spoon into 8 custard cups. Cover.

Freeze at least 4 hours.

Serves 8.

a strawberry a day...

Strawberries are high in vitamin C. Eight berries contain 130% of the recommended daily allowance of this vitamin.

APPROXIMATE PER SERVING: *102 calories; 4.7 grams of fat*

NOTES

Partito Italiano

Italy is known for its rich, flavorful cuisine. This theme puts a fun twist on Italian foods and traditions. Create the feeling of Tuscany and rustic Italy with a few simple decorations and delicious food. Plan this little Partito Italiano (Italian Party) anytime of the year.

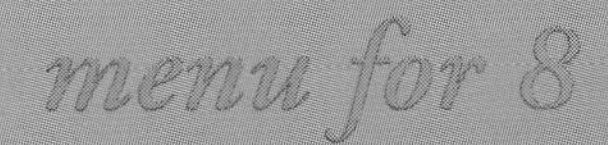

- Chianti-Grilled Mushrooms and Onions
- Iced Cappuccino
- Antipasto Salad
- Crostini
- Grilled Vegetables
- Linguini with Tomato, Basil, and Capers
- Dilled Carrots
- Tiramisu

Invitations

- Paste 4 × 4-inch squares of cream-colored card stock onto 5 × 5-inch pieces of burlap. Punch two holes approximately 1 inch from each other at the top of the card. Looping the raffia ribbon into the card from the back, tie a neat bow in the front center of the card.

- Edge white card stock with stamped grape shapes, a grape leaf design, lemons, or olives. Print or write party information on the front of the card.

- An alternative is to purchase commercial invitations with images of wine, fruits and vegetables, and Italian bread loaves.

Decorations

- Use a non-metallic gold or tobacco-colored burlap or cloth table covering. Carry through the motif you used for your invitations (grape leaf, lemons, or olives) by stamping or sponge painting the same images on the tablecloth.

- Many antique stores sell rustic Italian pottery serving pieces, which can be used for other occasions after the party.

- Wine, especially Chianti, enhances the Tuscany-inspired atmosphere. Disperse bottles of wine around the serving table if they are to be opened and consumed at dinner, or place them in a wine rack for decoration only.

- Place planters of fresh lavender and bowls of lemons, limes, and garlic bulbs in the foyer, kitchen area, or buffet. These make nice low centerpieces. Other decorating ideas include hanging garlic braids from the ceiling and arranging bottles and jars of marinated fruits and vegetables on tables. Many specialty shops carry a variety of marinated fruits and vegetables.

- Inexpensive grapevine wreaths, readily available at craft stores, can be hung or used to surround serving pieces. Use grapevine "ribbon" to hang artificial grape clusters and leaves from the ceiling.

Activities

- Bocce, one of the oldest games in history, is a favorite national pastime in Italy. Players of all ages can have a great time playing together. Bocce can really be played anywhere, but is easiest on a level surface. You will need to mark the front and the back of the court with chalk, tape, or paint.

  General equipment for bocce includes eight large balls (four marked to distinguish them from the others) and one smaller ball, which is called a *pallino*. Teams can consist of one, two, or four players. Brush up on instructions for playing bocce by consulting a book or researching the game on the Internet.

- An alternate activity is a short game of soccer.

Setting the Scene

- Consider playing arias and selections from famous Italian composers, such as those here. Or play a language tape and join your guests in learning Italian words and phrases.

  Musical selection possibilities:
  Madame Butterfly by Pucini / *The Best of Italian Opera* by various composers and performers / *The Three Tenors* performed by Carreras, Domingo, and Pavarotti / *Italian* produced by Easy Go (instructional language product) / *Romanza* by Andrea Bocelli

  Video selection possibilities:
  Cinema Paradiso / *Il Postino* (*The Postman*) / *The Godfather* / *The Godfather, Part II*

Chianti-Grilled Mushrooms and Onions

1 cup fat-free Italian dressing
1/2 cup Chianti or other red wine
1/2 tablespoon garlic, minced
Dash of salt and pepper
2 cups whole mushrooms
1 large Portabella mushroom cap, sliced into 2-inch pieces
2 medium red onions, quartered
2 medium sweet yellow onions, quartered

Mix Italian dressing, wine, garlic, and salt and pepper.

Toss vegetables with dressing mixture to coat, keeping mushrooms and onions separate. Marinate for 1 to 2 hours or longer.

Heat grill to medium-high heat.

Skewer vegetables (or cook in grilling basket to prevent small items from falling onto coals or heating element). Grill mushrooms for 1 to 2 minutes per side until tender and lightly browned, and grill onions 2 to 3 minutes per side.

Remove vegetables and arrange in separate piles on a large platter.

Serve with toothpicks.

Serves 8.

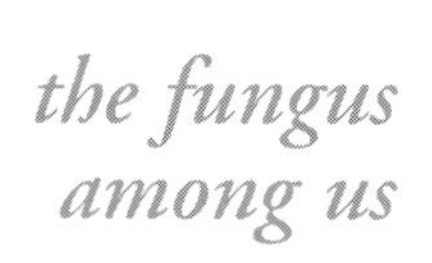

Mushrooms soak up water like sponges, then release it later while cooking. This can change the consistency of recipes. Try "dry-cleaning" your favorite fungus instead. You can find a mushroom brush with soft bristles at most kitchen stores. Lightly moisten the brush (or a rag) with water and gently wipe the mushrooms clean.

APPROXIMATE PER SERVING: *50 calories; 0 grams of fat*

Iced Cappuccino

4 cups freshly brewed espresso, cooled to room temperature
8 cups ice cubes
1 cup skim or 1% milk
3/4 cup superfine sugar or to taste
1 teaspoon cinnamon
Cinnamon for garnish

Blend all ingredients except cinnamon for garnish in a blender until smooth but still thick.

Divide mixture evenly between 8 glasses.

Sprinkle with cinnamon, if desired.

Makes approximately 11 cups.
Serves 8.

clearly cappuccino

Espresso is strong, dark coffee made by forcing steam through a special coffee blend. Traditional cappuccino is an Italian drink made by mixing milk foam with espresso and topping it with a dollop of steamed milk foam. • Around 1660, the Dutch Ambassador to China became the first person to mix coffee with milk. He was imitating the practice of adding milk to tea.

APPROXIMATE PER SERVING: *15 calories; 0 grams of fat*

Antipasto Salad

1 14-1/2-ounce can of artichoke hearts
1/4 cup each of assorted olives, such as black, Kalamata, or green
1/2 15-ounce can chickpeas
1/4 pound roasted red peppers
1/2 cup low-fat mozzarella cheese, cubed
1/2 cup baby corn
1/2 cup sun-dried tomatoes, softened in boiling water and chopped
1/4 cup turkey pepperoni, cubed or sliced
1/4 cup turkey salami, cubed or sliced
3/4 cup low-fat Italian or Caesar dressing
Dash of salt and pepper

Combine all ingredients in a large bowl. Mix well.
Makes approximately 16-1/2 cups.
Chill and serve.

Serves 8.

antipasto etymology

The Italian term antipasto means "before the pasta." A platter of antipasto can include hot or cold appetizers as varied as sun-dried tomatoes with tuna and spices; a salad of potatoes, apples, and cheese; stewed peppers, roasted stuffed tomatoes; and marinated eggplant.

APPROXIMATE PER SERVING: *470 calories; 11 grams of fat*

Crostini

Unlike herbs that contain a lot of moisture, rosemary doesn't change significantly in volume or flavor when dried, so use the same amount of either when rosemary is called for.

1 loaf Italian bread, sliced into 1/2-inch rounds
1 garlic clove, peeled, cut in half
Cooking spray
1/2 tablespoon garlic salt
1 tablespoon rosemary
1 tablespoon olive oil

Preheat broiler.

Arrange bread slices on cookie sheet. Rub each round with half of a garlic clove. Discard clove.

Spray rounds with cooking spray, then sprinkle with garlic salt and rosemary.

Drizzle with olive oil and broil 2 to 3 minutes or until lightly browned.

Serves 8.

versatile crostini

Serve crostini as a delicious and simple side on its own, or top lightly oiled crostini with a mixture of chopped tomatoes and black olives; goat cheese and chives; roasted garlic; figs and gorgonzola; or anything other flavors that appeal to you.

APPROXIMATE PER SERVING: *90 calories; 2.5 grams of fat*

Grilled Vegetables

1 cup fat-free Italian dressing
1 small eggplant, sliced lengthwise into 1/2-inch slices
2 medium zucchini, sliced lengthwise into 1/2-inch slices
2 medium summer squash, sliced lengthwise into 1/2-inch slices
2 red peppers, cored, seeded, and sliced into 1/2-inch rings
2 green peppers, cored, seeded, and sliced into 1/2-inch rings
2 yellow peppers, cored, seeded, and sliced into 1/2-inch rings
1/2 head fennel, leaves removed, cut into 4-inch pieces
1 tablespoon garlic salt

Toss vegetables with Italian dressing to coat, keeping each type of vegetable separate.

Heat grill to medium-high heat.

Skewer vegetables (or cook in grilling basket to prevent small items from falling onto coals or heating element).

Grill until tender and lightly browned:

1 to 2 minutes per side for peppers

2 to 3 minutes per side for eggplant and squashes

3 to 4 minutes per side for fennel.

Sprinkle with garlic salt while cooking.

Remove vegetables from grill and place on a large platter, separating each type of vegetables.

Serves 8.

Fresh fennel, available from fall through spring, is rich in vitamin A and contains a fair amount of calcium, phosphorus, and potassium. When picking fennel, look for clean, crisp bulbs and greenery with no signs of browning. Tightly wrap in a plastic bag and refrigerate for up to 5 days.

APPROXIMATE PER SERVING: *80 calories; 0 grams of fat*

Linguini with Tomato, Basil, and Capers

Immerse tomatoes in boiling water for a few minutes so you'll be able to remove the skins more easily. This is called blanching.

4 tomatoes, peeled, seeded, and coarsely chopped
1 cup fresh basil, coarsely chopped
3 tablespoons olive oil, divided
1/3 cup onion, finely chopped
1/2 cup carrot, finely chopped
1/2 cup celery, finely chopped
3 cloves garlic, crushed
1 3-1/4-ounce jar capers, drained and rinsed
3 tablespoons vinegar
Salt and pepper to taste
2 pounds spinach or whole-wheat linguini, uncooked

In a large pan of boiling water, cook linguini according to package directions. Drain.

Meanwhile, mix tomatoes and basil in a bowl. Set aside.

Heat 1 tablespoon of oil in a skillet over low heat. Add onion and sauté until translucent, about 2 to 3 minutes. Add carrot, celery, and garlic and sauté for another minute.

Add tomato mixture and simmer, uncovered, for 20 minutes. Add capers, vinegar, salt, and pepper.

Drizzle remaining olive oil on linguini, tossing to coat.

Place linguini onto a large serving platter and top with sauce.

Serves 8.

If you don't plan to use fresh basil the day you buy it, don't keep it in the refrigerator. Storing basil below 48°F will make the herb turn black. Store fresh basil as you would treat a plant cutting, placing the stems in a glass of water.

APPROXIMATE PER SERVING: *194 calories; 6 grams of fat*

Dilled Carrots

2 pounds carrots, sliced
1/3 cup fresh parsley, chopped
1/4 cup vegetable or chicken broth
3 tablespoons white wine vinegar
1 tablespoon olive oil
2 teaspoons granulated sugar
3 tablespoons fresh dill, chopped or 1 teaspoon dried dillweed
Salt and pepper to taste

In a saucepan over medium heat, steam carrots until tender-crisp. Drain and place carrots in a large bowl.

Combine parsley, broth, vinegar, olive oil, sugar, dill, salt, and pepper in a small bowl and mix well.

Pour mixture over warm carrots. Marinate in refrigerator for several hours.

Serves 8.

the real dill

The dill plant's feathery green leaves are called dill weed. Dill weed is commercially available either fresh or dried. Dried dill weed doesn't retain the strong flavor of fresh dill. Add fresh dill toward the end of your dish's cooking time, however, because cooking it diminishes its scent.

APPROXIMATE PER SERVING: *67 calories; 3 grams of fat*

Tiramisu

Shave chocolate quickly and easily by using a vegetable peeler.

1 cup strong coffee or espresso
2 tablespoons sugar
2 teaspoons cornstarch
1 large box instant chocolate pudding mix
2 cups skim milk
1 cup part skim ricotta cheese
3 cups fat-free whipped topping, divided
Half of a 13-ounce fat-free pound cake, cut into 2-inch cubes
1-1/2-ounce piece bittersweet chocolate, shaved, for garnish

TO PREPARE SYRUP: In small saucepan over medium-high heat, bring coffee or espresso and sugar to a boil.

Add cornstarch and cook 5 to 6 minutes or until thickened.

Remove coffee syrup mixture from heat and cool.

TO PREPARE CHOCOLATE: Prepare pudding according to package directions, but use only 2 cups of milk instead of 4. Chill.

TO PREPARE RICOTTA: Mix together ricotta cheese and 1 cup of whipped topping.

TO ASSEMBLE TIRAMISU: Press pound cake cubes into bottom of a large glass bowl or trifle dish. Pour coffee syrup evenly over cake.

Spread ricotta mixture over cake smoothly. Spread chocolate pudding mixture on top of ricotta layer. Top with remaining whipped topping.

Sprinkle with chocolate shavings.

Chill at least 1 hour before serving to allow the flavors to meld.

Serves 8.

tiramisu who?

Tiramisu is a traditional Italian dessert that is sometimes compared to a trifle, although its texture and flavor are much lighter than an everyday trifle. Literally translated, tiramisu means "carry me up," which is what some fans of this dessert feel happens when they eat it.

APPROXIMATE PER SERVING: *330 calories; 2 grams of fat*

NOTES

Taste of Nations Dinner

This theme, featuring dishes from regions around the world, is a great opportunity for friends to have fun eating food from varied cultures.

The unusual mix of flavors suggested here is sure to keep your guests' attention without overwhelming them. You can customize the menu by serving dishes reflecting your or your guests' heritage or adding favorite ethnic dishes to those listed here.

Offer fresh parsley and/or mint so your friends may cleanse their palettes in between dishes and prepare for the next flavorful dish.

menu for 8

- Middle Eastern Baked Falafel
- Iced Turkish Coffee
- Artichoke Hearts Toscana
- Indian Curried Carrot Soup
- Hungarian Chicken
- Greek Zucchini
- Pears Hélène

Invitations

- Send out commercially available white or colored card stock invitations bordered with flags of many nations.

- Or use plain folded card stock and print the words for "party," "dinner," or "eat" in different languages on the front. Print party information (in English) inside.

Decorations

- Display international flags and travel posters. Use brightly colored napkins, plates, and tablecloths.

- Decorate food dishes with international flag toothpicks, which are commercially available, or use national colors to label a tent card identifying each dish.

Activity

- Hang a large world map on the wall. Give guests colored dot stickers to place on the map showing where their families are originally from. See how many countries and states party guests represent.

- Learn traditional international dances by following an instruction tape or following instructions from a knowledgeable guest.

Setting the Scene

- Play an assortment of international music. A sampler of world music should do the trick:

  World Music by various artists
  World Music Sampler volumes by various artists
  World Music Collection by various artists

Middle Eastern Baked Falafel

Serve each falafel patty in a miniature pita with lettuce and tomato.

2 15-ounce cans cooked chickpeas (approximately 4 cups), drained
4 medium garlic cloves, minced
2 teaspoons cumin
1 teaspoon turmeric
1 teaspoon salt
1/2 cup finely minced onion or 6 minced scallions
1/4 cup minced parsley
1/4 cup water
1 tablespoon lemon juice
Dash of cayenne
1/3 cup flour
Cooking spray

Preheat oven to 400°F.

Process all ingredients except flour and cooking spray in a food processor until combined. Add flour and process until combined.

Spray baking sheet with nonstick spray.

Form the batter into tablespoon-sized balls, then flatten and place on baking sheet.

Bake falafel patties for 20 to 25 minutes or until golden brown, turning once.

Serves 8.

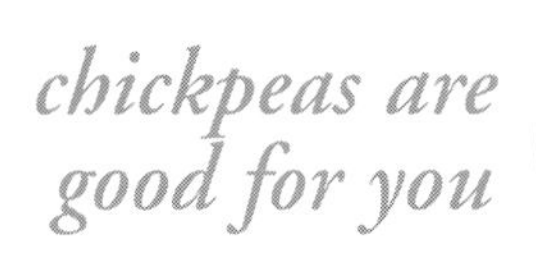

Chickpeas—a staple of Middle Eastern diet—are a good source of protein. They are also rich in calcium and iron and are an excellent source of fiber. • Easy Lunch: Heat chickpeas, drizzle them with a little extra virgin olive oil, and season to taste with salt and pepper. Add a tossed salad for a fresh, simple lunch.

APPROXIMATE PER SERVING: *120 calories; 2 grams of fat*

Iced Turkish Coffee

We've toned down Turkish coffee—traditionally a very strong drink—by adding low-fat milk and serving it over ice. You might want to serve this coffee with dessert.

4 cups 1% milk
1/4 cup sugar
24 whole cardamom pods, crushed
4 cups strong brewed coffee, chilled

In a small saucepan combine milk, sugar, and cardamom. Bring the mixture to a boil, stirring until the sugar is dissolved. Allow to cool.

Strain through a sieve set over a small pitcher. Stir in the coffee and chill, covered, for 30 minutes or until cold.

Divide the coffee between 8 glasses filled with ice cubes.

Makes approximately 7 cups.
Serves 8.

turkish coffee

Turkish coffee is very strong coffee made with sugar as well as spices like cardamom and cinnamon. It's usually brewed in a very specific way: it's brought to a boil three times, and allowed to cool briefly in between. It's made in a special long-handled pots and served in tiny cups.

APPROXIMATE PER SERVING: *60 calories; 1.3 grams of fat*

Artichoke Hearts Toscana

Use sun-dried tomatoes that are dry-packed in cellophane instead of those packed in oil. Follow directions for reconstituting them (plumping them up in hot water) before using them in this Italian recipe.

2 tablespoons olive oil
2 cloves of garlic, minced
1 large onion, chopped
1 pound mushrooms, sliced
2 ounces prosciutto, chopped
1/2 teaspoon dried sage
1/4 cup reconstituted sun-dried tomatoes, chopped
3/4 cup dry white wine
1/2 cup water
2 14-ounce cans whole artichoke hearts
Salt and pepper to taste

In a frying pan over medium-high heat, combine oil, garlic, onion, mushrooms, and prosciutto. Cook 15 to 20 minutes or until onion is golden and mushrooms are brown and glazed, stirring occasionally.

Add sage, tomatoes, wine, water, and artichokes. Bring to a boil.

Cover and simmer approximately 45 minutes or until artichokes are tender when pierced, stirring occasionally.

Season to taste with salt and pepper.

Serves 8.

getting to the heart of artichokes

An artichoke is really a thistle flower bud. When purchasing fresh artichokes, choose dark green, heavy artichokes with leaves that are tightly closed. Try to use fresh artichokes right away, or refrigerate unwashed artichokes in a plastic bag for up to 4 days. Artichokes contain some potassium and vitamin A.

APPROXIMATE PER SERVING: *135 calories; 5 grams of fat*

Indian Curried Carrot Soup

Be careful when puréeing hot liquids in the blender. Blend in small batches so liquid doesn't overflow. This soup may also be served chilled.

2 tablespoons corn oil margarine
8 cups carrots, chopped
2 cups onion, chopped
1 teaspoon curry powder
1 teaspoon cumin
1 teaspoon coriander
10 cups water
1 teaspoon salt (optional)
1/2 teaspoon pepper
2 cups low-fat cottage cheese
2 cups 1% milk
2 teaspoons fresh lemon juice
1 cup green bell pepper, chopped
1 cup fresh parsley, chopped

Melt margarine in a large stockpot over low heat. Add carrots and onion and sauté for 5 minutes, adding curry powder, cumin, and coriander. Add water, salt, and pepper. Bring to a boil over medium-high heat, reduce heat, and cover partially. Simmer for 15 minutes.

Pour carrot mixture into a blender and process until puréed. Return mixture to stockpot.

Place cottage cheese, milk, and lemon juice in a blender and process until smooth. Pour into carrot mixture.

Heat to serving temperature over low heat and ladle into soup bowls.

Garnish with green pepper and parsley. Soup may be served chilled.

Serves 8.

carrots and health

Carrots provide 330% of your recommended daily allowance of Vitamin A. They are also very high in phytochemicals such as antioxidants, flavonoids, and carotenoids, including beta-carotene. • Many people purchase carrots with the tops still attached. However, the carrot greenery deprives the roots (the carrot) of moisture and vitamins. Remove the greenery to store them longer. Revive limp carrots in a bowl of ice water. • Do not store carrots with apples; apples emit an ethylene gas that causes carrots to taste bitter.

APPROXIMATE PER SERVING: *167 calories; 6 grams of fat*

Hungarian Chicken

Hungarian cuisine is traditionally rich in fat and calories. Here we've departed from cooking with lard or rendered bacon fat, which are traditional in Hungarian dishes.

3 tablespoons corn oil or safflower oil
4 chicken breasts, skinned, boned, and cut into 1-1/2-inch pieces
2 cups fresh mushrooms, sliced
1 cup onion, chopped
1 cup chicken broth
2 tablespoons paprika
2 teaspoons fresh dill or 1/2 teaspoon dried dillweed
1/2 teaspoon pepper
5 cups uncooked egg noodles
1/4 cup cold water
1/4 cup cornstarch
2 cups low-fat plain yogurt

Heat oil in a large skillet over medium heat. Add chicken, mushrooms, and onion and sauté over medium-high heat until tender. Add broth, paprika, dill, and pepper. Cover, reduce heat, and simmer for 10 minutes or until chicken is tender.

Cook noodles according to package directions using unsalted water, then drain.

Blend water and cornstarch in a small bowl, then stir into chicken mixture. Cook for 1 minute, stirring constantly. Remove from heat.

Stir in yogurt.

Serve over noodles.

Serves 8.

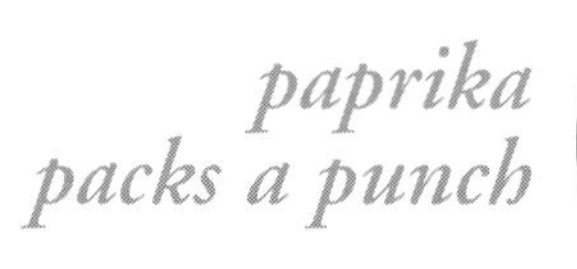

Paprika is a powder made by grinding sweet red pepper pods. Its flavor can range from sweet and mild to hot and strong. Look in ethnic markets for Hungarian paprika, which is often considered the highest quality and most pungent paprika available. Spicy paprika will be labeled eros; mild paprika will be labeled edesmes.

APPROXIMATE PER SERVING: *340 calories; 9 grams of fat*

Greek Zucchini

8 small zucchini, scored lengthwise with fork
2/3 cup water
1 tablespoon corn oil margarine
1 medium onion, chopped
1 clove garlic, chopped
4 ripe tomatoes, peeled and chopped
Salt and pepper to taste

In a large saucepan, cook zucchini in water over medium heat just until tender. Remove pan from heat and set aside.

In a skillet, sauté onion and garlic in margarine until tender. Add tomatoes and cook until soft. Season to taste with salt and pepper.

Drain zucchini and arrange on a serving plate.

Spoon tomato mixture over each piece of zucchini.

Serves 8.

zucchini in a flash

Keep in mind that large zucchini are less tender than smaller squash. Look for zucchini with dark green, shiny, firm skin. • Here's a simple zucchini side: Cook a pound of zucchini in 1/4 cup of vegetable stock, adding five sliced green onions and salt and pepper to taste. Simmer 5 minutes and stir in a tablespoon of lemon juice before serving.

APPROXIMATE PER SERVING: *53 calories; 1 gram of fat*

Pears Hélène

Pears are featured in many delicious French desserts, including pear flan, pears in red wine, and baked pears. Here we've simmered the pears and topped them with frozen yogurt.

8 pears
4 cups water
4 teaspoons lemon juice
1-1/3 cups sugar
1 tablespoon vanilla extract
1 pint each vanilla and chocolate low-fat frozen yogurt
Grated chocolate for garnish

Peel, core, and halve pears.

In large saucepan over medium heat, bring water, lemon juice, and sugar to simmer. Add pears and simmer for 10 minutes. Add vanilla extract.

Cool pears and syrup mixture.

Drain pears, then fill pear halves with a scoop each of vanilla and chocolate frozen yogurt and top with grated chocolate.

Serves 8.

ripening pears

To ripen pears, store them at room temperature in a sealed plastic bag with a ripe banana. Refrigerate ripe pears until you're ready to use them.

APPROXIMATE PER SERVING: *280 calories; 2 grams of fat*

NOTES

NOTES

The American Cancer Society's Commitment to Promoting Healthy Living

An estimated one-third of all cancer deaths that occur in the United States are related to nutrition and physical activity factors. If you don't smoke, the most important ways you can improve your health and reduce your risk (not only of cancer, but heart disease and diabetes as well) are by eating a healthy diet, being physically active, and maintaining a healthy weight. The good news is that cancer, heart disease, and diabetes are largely preventable through healthy lifestyle choices. You can take steps each and every day to reduce your risk of these diseases, all the while feeling better, looking better, and getting the energy you need to get through your busy days.

And that's what *Celebrate!* is all about—providing you with delicious and fun ways to eat better, be more active, and promote healthy living to your family and friends.

The American Cancer Society's Nutrition and Physical Activity Guidelines for Cancer Prevention

Eating a healthy diet, being physically active, and maintaining a healthy weight can promote health and reduce cancer risk at any age. To reduce your risk of cancer, the American Cancer Society offers these recommendations:

(1) Eat a variety of healthy foods, with an emphasis on plant sources.

Eat five or more servings of a variety of vegetables and fruits each day.

- Include vegetables and fruits at every meal and as snacks.
- Eat a variety of vegetables and fruits.
- Limit French fries, snack chips, and other fried vegetable products.
- Choose 100-percent juice if you drink fruit or vegetable juices.

Choose whole grains over processed (refined) grains and sugars.

- Choose whole-grain rice, bread, pasta, and cereals.
- Limit your consumption of refined carbohydrates, including pastries, sweetened cereals, soft drinks, and sugars.

Limit your consumption of red meats, especially those high in fat and processed.

- Choose fish, poultry, or beans as an alternative to beef, pork, and lamb.
- When you eat meat, select lean cuts and smaller portions.
- Prepare meat by baking, broiling, or poaching rather than frying or charbroiling.

Choose foods that help you maintain a healthy weight.

- Choose food low in fat, calories, and sugar, and avoid large portion sizes.

- Eat smaller portions of high-calorie foods. Be aware that "low-fat" or "nonfat" does not mean "low-calorie," and that low-fat cakes, cookies, and similar foods are often high in calories.
- Substitute vegetables, fruits, and other low-calorie foods for calorie-dense foods such as French fries, cheeseburgers, pizza, ice cream, doughnuts, and other sweets.

(2) **Adopt a physically active lifestyle.**

- Adults: Be active for at least 30 minutes on 5 or more days per week; being even more active is probably better.
- Children and adolescents: Be active for at least 60 minutes on 5 or more days per week.

(3) **Maintain a healthful weight throughout life.**

- Balance the number of calories you take in with your level of physical activity.
- Lose weight if you are currently overweight or obese.

(4) **If you drink alcoholic beverages, limit your consumption.**

- Men: Limit alcohol consumption to no more than two drinks per day. Women: Limit consumption to no more than one drink per day.
- A drink is defined as 12 ounces of regular beer, 5 ounces of wine, or 1½ ounces of 80-proof distilled spirits.

Although smoking is less socially acceptable now than it has been in the past, some of your guests may wish to smoke at your get-together. Smoking poses a health risk to smokers and nonsmokers alike. Nonsmokers who are exposed to environmental tobacco smoke (second-hand smoke) absorb nicotine and other compounds just as smokers do. The American Cancer Society warns against the dangers of tobacco, which is responsible for one-third of cancer deaths. Ask your guests to keep your get-together smoke-free.

Staying healthy requires more than eating well and being active. Getting enough rest, managing stress, and having regular physical checkups are also crucial to ensuring good health. Checkups are especially important for early detection of cancer and heart disease. If you have special diet or physical activity concerns, check with your healthcare provider for more specific information about incorporating lifestyle changes.

For more information about the importance of nutrition, physical activity, and weight control, or for information about quitting smoking or the dangers of tobacco, call 800-ACS-2345 or visit www.cancer.org.

RESOURCES

For information about nutrition, physical activity, and weight control, contact the American Cancer Society at 800-ACS-2345.

Resources for Nutrition and Health Promotion

Choices for Good Health: Guidelines for Diet, Nutrition, and Cancer Prevention, ACS Pamphlet, call 800-ACS-2345 to obtain a copy

Living Smart: The American Cancer Society's Guide to Eating Healthy and Being Active, ACS Pamphlet, call 800-ACS-2345 to obtain a copy

Cooking Smart: The American Cancer Society's Recipe for Quick and Easy Healthy Eating from Your Very Own Kitchen, ACS Pamphlet, call 800-ACS-2345 to obtain a copy

Eat Smart with Fruits and Vegetables, ACS Pamphlet, call 800-ACS-2345 to obtain a copy

Smart Steps: The American Cancer Society Guide to Being More Physically Active, ACS Pamphlet, call 800-ACS-2345 to obtain a copy

Taking Control, ACS Pamphlet, call 800-ACS-2345 to obtain a copy

The American Dietetic Association (ADA)
120 South Riverside Plaza
Chicago, IL 60606
Toll-Free: 800-877-1600 (main number); 800-366-1655 (for information and dietitian referral)
Web site: http://www.eatright.org

The ADA operates a consumer nutrition hotline, which provides referrals to registered dietitians in local areas including dietitians specializing in oncology nutrition. Their web site contains information on diet and nutrition and a registered dietitian locator service.

The American Heart Association (AHA)
7272 Greenville Avenue
Dallas, TX 75231-4596
Phone: 214-373-6300
Web site: http://www.americanheart.org

The AHA web site offers information about cardiovascular diseases including heart diseases and stroke, and suggests ways to reduce the risk of developing these diseases. The site also includes general family health resources, such as information about nutrition, exercise, and children's health.

National Cancer Institute (NCI)
NCI Public Inquiries Office
Room 3036A6116
Executive Boulevard, MSC 8322
Bethesda, MD 20892-2580
Toll-free: 800-4-CANCER
Web site: http://www.cancer.gov

This government agency provides information on cancer research, diagnosis, and treatment to people with cancer, caregivers, and health care providers. NCI also maintains a listing of current clinical trails.

National Cancer Institute (NCI)
5 A Day for Better Health Program
Center for Strategic Dissemination
6130 Executive Boulevard, EPN 4050
MSC 7332
Bethesda, MD 20892
Toll-free: 800-4-CANCER
Web site: http://5aday.gov

The national 5 A Day for Better Health Program gives Americans a simple message —eat 5 or more servings of fruits and vegetables every day for better health. The program is jointly sponsored by the National Cancer Institute in the US Department of Health and Human Services and the Produce for Better Health foundation, a nonprofit consumer education foundation representing the fruit and vegetable industry.

U.S. Department of Agriculture (USDA) Food and Nutrition Information Center (FNIC)
National Agricultural Library, Room 105
10301 Baltimore Avenue
Beltsville, MD 20705-2351
Phone: 301-504-5719 (main); 301-504-5414 for inquiries to dietitians and nutritionists
Web site: http://www.nal.usda.gov/fnic

The USDA's Food and Nutrition Information Center is an information center for the National Agricultural Library. FNIC materials and services include dietitians and nutritionists available to answer inquiries, publications on food and nutrition, and resource lists and bibliographies.

Conversion Tables for Cooking

Kitchen Measurements

3 teaspoons = 1 tablespoon
4 tablespoons = 1/4 cup
5 tablespoons + 1 teaspoon = 1/3 cup
8 tablespoons = 1/2 cup
12 tablespoons = 3/4 cup
16 tablespoons = 1 cup
2 cups = 1 pint
4 cups = 1 quart
2 pints = 1 quart
4 quarts = 1 gallon

U.S. to Metric Cooking Measurement Equivalents

Capacity

1 teaspoon = 5 milliliters
1 tablespoon = 15 milliliters
1/2 cup = 120 milliliters
1 cup = 240 milliliters
2 cups (1 pint) = 470 milliliters
4 cups (1 quart) = 0.95 liter
4 quarts (1 gallon) = 3.8 liters

Weight

1 ounce = 28 grams
1 pound = 454 grams

A

Activities, vi
- Backyard Beach Barbecue, 61
- Book Club Supper, 27
- Country Fair Canning Party, 124
- Croquet Classic, 99
- Game Night, 165
- Get Your Hands Dirty Garden Party, 17
- Home on the Range Hoedown, 49
- Jamaican Jam, 73
- Life is a Bowl of Cherries Celebration, 39
- Mount Olympus Greek Party, 113
- On the "Green" Golf Party, 3
- Partito Italiano, 223
- Post-Holiday Blues Party, 189
- Pre-Hike Breakfast, 139
- Pumpkin-Carving Contest, 153
- Salsa Party, 85
- Season's Greetings Holiday Affair, 176–177
- "Souper" Bowl Bash, 201
- Taste of Nations Dinner, 235
- This Must Be Love Valentine's Day Dinner, 211

Alcohol and cancer, 246
American Dietetic Association, 247
American Heart Association, 247
Antipasto Salad, 226
Appetizers
- *Basil and Tomato Bruschetta*, 4
- *Chianti-Grilled Mushrooms and Onions*, 224
- *Creamy Double-O Relish*, 130
- *Crispy Shrimp Sensations*, 41
- *Dilled Salmon Mousse*, 100
- *Green Chile Artichoke Dip*, 190
- *Heavenly Hummus*, 114
- *Jerk Shrimp with Berry Sauce*, 74
- *Kick-Off Crunch*, 202
- *Make-Your-Own Cereal and On-the-Trail Mix*, 148
- *Mini Bean Croquettes with Tomato-Anchovy Dip*, 101–102
- *Scary Spiced Popcorn*, 154
- *Spinach and Tomato Quesadilla Trees*, 178
- *Turkey Sausage Bites with Sweet Hot Mustard Sauce*, 155
- *Zucchini Bites*, 40
- *See also* Dips; Fruits; Salads; Vegetables

Apples
- *Baklava with Fruit Compote*, 121
- *Caramel Dipping Sauce*, 127
- *Epilogue Praline-Apple Crisp*, 35
- *Sparkling Sunset Citrus Spritzer*, 142
- tasting, 124

Apricots
- *Flip Juice*, 168
- *Herb-Rubbed Pork Loin with Apricot-Pecan Stuffing*, 157–158
- *Mulled Punch*, 128

Artichoke Hearts Toscana, 238
Artichokes
- *Antipasto Salad*, 226
- *Artichoke Hearts Toscana*, 238
- *Eggplant Pizza*, 171
- *Green Chile Artichoke Dip*, 190
- *Marinated Artichoke and Potato Salad*, 22

Asparagus, 18
Avocados, 105–106

B

Backyard Beach Barbecue
- activities, 61
- decorations, 60
- invitations, 60
- *Lemon Watermelon Slush*, 68
- *Red Bliss Potato Salad*, 65
- *Red, Yellow, and Green Dip with Parmesan Pita Triangles*, 62
- *Seaside Punch*, 63
- setting the scene, 61
- *Skewered Shrimp, Chicken, and Pineapple with Honey Orange Dipping Sauce*, 64
- *Summer Fruit Salad with Poppy Seed Dressing*, 66
- *White Bean Salad*, 67

Baked Sweet Potato Wedges, 78
Baklava with Fruit Compote, 121
Banana Custard, 80
Bananas
- *Banana Custard*, 80
- *Energizing Smoothie*, 140
- *Tropical Fruit Display*, 79

Barbecue. *See* Grilling
Basil and Tomato Bruschetta, 4

Beans
black, 9, 77, 89, 90–91, 93, 166, 182
Black Bean Cakes, 9
Black Bean-Filled Sweet Potato Biscuits with Queso Fresco, 90–91
Black Beans and Rice with Papaya and Red Onions, 77
Breakfast Burritos, 145–146
cannellini, 67
Caribbean Rice and Beans, 93
Confetti Beans and Rice, 182
Corn, Onion, Red Pepper, White Bean, and Cilantro Salsa, 86
Crunchy Green Beans with Caramelized Onions, 44
Green Chile Artichoke Dip, 190
kidney, 166
Mini Bean Croquettes with Tomato-Anchovy Dip, 101–102
Ranch Beans, 53
Sideline Chicken Chili, 205
Three Bean Creole Dip, 166
white, 67, 86, 126, 166
See also Vegetables
Beef
and cancer prevention, 245
Halfback Beef Burgundy Soup, 206
Rosemary Beef with Shallot Sauce, 216
Texas Dry-Rub Barbecue, 54
Beets
Best-Seller Beet and Orange Salad, 31
Halfback Beef Burgundy Soup, 206
Ruby Red Beets with Fennel, 218
Best-Seller Beet and Orange Salad, 31
Bibliophile Bread, 28–29
Bitters, 43
Black Bean Cakes, 9
Black Bean-Filled Sweet Potato Biscuits with Queso Fresco, 90–91
Black Beans and Rice with Papaya and Red Onions, 77
Blanching, 18
Bloody Mary Mix, 5
Blue Ribbon Sun-Dried Tomato Dip, 126
Blue Storm, 191
Blueberries
Blueberry Peach Crisp, 134
Couscous with Almonds, Dried Blueberries, and Parmesan Cheese, 194
Lemon Cake with Brandied Blueberry Sauce, 196–197
Book Club Supper
activities, 27
Best-Seller Beet and Orange Salad, 31
Bibliophile Bread, 28–29
Cliffhanger Cappuccino Coolers, 30
decorations, 26
invitations, 26
Novel New Potatoes and Sugar Snap Peas, 34
Page-Turner Tuna Steaks with Ginger-Lime Crust, 33
"Read" Pepper Soup with Sour Cream and Chives, 32
setting the scene, 27
Breads and grains
Basil and Tomato Bruschetta, 4
Bibliophile Bread, 28–29
Black Bean-Filled Sweet Potato Biscuits with Queso Fresco, 90–91
bruschetta, 4
bulghur, 169
Couscous with Almonds, Dried Blueberries, and Parmesan Cheese, 194
Cowboy Cornbread, 51
crostini, 67, 227
muffins, 143–144, 147
pita, 62, 114
Polenta Hearts with Roasted Red Pepper and Olive Tapenade, 212–213
Pumpkin Oat Muffins, 147
Red, Yellow, and Green Dip with Parmesan Pita Triangles, 62
Rise 'n Shine English Muffins, 143–144
See also Side dishes
Breakfast Burritos, 145–146
Brown Rice Pilaf, 45
Bruschetta, 4
Buffets, v–vi
Bulghur, 169
Buttermilk, 24, 131, 147, 172–173
Buttermilk Chocolate Drops, 24
Buttermilk Garlic Mashed Potatoes, 217

C

Cabbage

Country Coleslaw, 131

Jicama Slaw, 92

Tri-Colored Jalapeño Slaw, 55

Caesar Salad, 204

Cancer

and alcohol, 245–246

and exercise, 245

and nutrition, 245–246

resources, 246–247

and smoking, 246

types of common, 246

Cannellini beans, 67

Canning, 124–125

Cantaloupes

Glorious Fruit Salad, 141

Minted Melon Balls, 23

Capers, 229

Caramel Dipping Sauce, 127

Caribbean Rice and Beans, 93

Carrots

Black Bean-Filled Sweet Potato Biscuits with Queso Fresco, 90–91

Dilled Carrots, 230

Harvest Rice, 160

Hearty Veggie Alphabet Soup, 181

Indian Curried Carrot Soup, 239

Julienned Carrot and Celery Orzo, 104

Linguini with Tomato, Basil, and Capers, 229

Round 'Em Up Oatmeal Carrot Bars, 57

Scrumptious Carrot Cake, 172–173

Tri-Colored Jalapeño Slaw, 55

Celery

Bloody Mary Mix, 5

Caribbean Rice and Beans, 93

Dilled Salmon Mousse, 100

Herb-Rubbed Pork Loin with Apricot-Pecan Stuffing, 157–158

Julienned Carrot and Celery Orzo, 104

Linguini with Tomato, Basil, and Capers, 229

Red Bliss Potato Salad, 65

Cereals, 148

Cheery Cherry Parfaits, 46

Cheese

blue, 193

cheddar, 145–146, 178

cottage, 100, 239

cream, 32, 115, 127, 130, 132–133, 172–173, 178, 208, 216

feta, 90–91, 118, 120, 169, 212–213

Mixed Greens with Assorted Vegetables, Fruits, Cheese, and Other Toppings, 11

mozzarella, 93, 107, 226

Parmesan, 62, 132–133, 143–144, 154, 159, 171, 190, 194, 204, 207

prosciutto, 238

queso fresco, 90–91

ricotta, 107, 208

Swiss, 170

Cherries

Cheery Cherry Parfaits, 46

Cherry Limeade, 42

Roast Turkey Breast with Sour Cherry Sauce, 43

Seaside Punch, 63

Cherry Limeade, 42

Chianti-Grilled Mushrooms and Onions, 224

Chicken

and cancer prevention, 245

Curried Chicken Salad, 21

Greek Chicken with Tomatoes, Peppers, Olives, and Feta, 118

ground, 155

Hungarian Chicken, 240

"I Got the Blues" Chicken, 193

Mexican Chicken Salad, 89

Sideline Chicken Chili, 205

Skewered Shrimp, Chicken, and Pineapple with Honey Orange Dipping Sauce, 64

Spiced Chicken Breast, 6

See also Turkey

Chickpeas

Antipasto Salad, 226

Heavenly Hummus, 114

Middle Eastern Baked Falafel, 236

Mini Bean Croquettes with Tomato-Anchovy Dip, 101–102

Chiles, 190

Chilled Asparagus with Horseradish-Dill Dipping Sauce, 18

Chocolate

Buttermilk Chocolate Drops, 24
Fourth Quarter Chocolate Cheesecake, 208
Hot Cocoa, 179
Pears Hélène, 242
Tiramisu, 231
Cliffhanger Cappuccino Coolers, 30
Coconut-Rum Salmon, 76
Coconuts
Coconut-Rum Salmon, 76
Golf Ball Cookies, 13
"Snow"-Dusted Fruit, 180
Coffee
Cliffhanger Cappuccino Coolers, 30
Iced Cappuccino, 225
Iced Turkish Coffee, 237
Tiramisu, 231
See also Drinks
Confetti Beans and Rice, 182
Conversion tables for cooking, 248
Cookies. *See* Desserts
Corn
Antipasto Salad, 226
Corn, Onion, Red Pepper, White Bean, and Cilantro Salsa, 86
County Corn on the Cob, 56
Cowboy Cornbread, 51
Green Chile Artichoke Dip, 190
Hearty Veggie Alphabet Soup, 181
Scary Spiced Popcorn, 154
Sideline Chicken Chili, 205
Corn, Onion, Red Pepper, White Bean, and Cilantro Salsa, 86
Country Coleslaw, 131
Country Fair Canning Party
activities, 124
Blue Ribbon Sun-Dried Tomato Dip, 126
Blueberry Peach Crisp, 134
canning, 124–125
Caramel Dipping Sauce, 127
Country Coleslaw, 131
Creamy Double-O Relish, 130
decorations, 124
Farm-Fresh Deviled Eggs, 129
Harvest Ham Primavera, 132–133
invitations, 124
Mulled Punch, 128
setting the scene, 125
Couscous with Almonds, Dried Blueberries, and Parmesan Cheese, 194
Cowboy Cornbread, 51
Cranberries
Flip Juice, 168
Hot Spiced Cider, 156
Mulled Punch, 128
Roast Turkey Breast with Sour Cherry Sauce, 43
Seaside Punch, 63
Valentine Spritzers, 214
Creamy Double-O Relish, 130
Creole seasoning, 166
Crispy Shrimp Sensations, 41
Croquet Classic
activities, 99
decorations, 98
Dilled Salmon Mousse, 100
invitations, 98
Julienned Carrot and Celery Orzo, 104
Mini Bean Croquettes with Tomato-Anchovy Dip, 101–102
Seared Sesame Scallops with Avocado Sauce, 105–106
setting the scene, 99
Summer Strawberry Shortcake, 108
Zucchini and Squash Tart, 107
Crostini, 67, 227
Crunchy Green Beans with Caramelized Onions, 44
Cucumbers
Cucumber Yogurt Dip, 115
Greek Salad, 120
Curried Chicken Salad, 21

D

Decorations
Backyard Beach Barbecue, 60
Book Club Supper, 26
Country Fair Canning Party, 124
Croquet Classic, 98
Game Night, 164
Get Your Hands Dirty Garden Party, 16–17
Home on the Range Hoedown, 48
Jamaican Jam, 72
Life is a Bowl of Cherries Celebration, 38

Mount Olympus Greek Party, 112
On the "Green" Golf Party, 2
Partito Italiano, 222
Post-Holiday Blues Party, 188
Pre-Hike Breakfast, 138
Pumpkin-Carving Contest, 152
Salsa Party, 84
Season's Greetings Holiday Affair, 176
"Souper" Bowl Bash, 200
Taste of Nations Dinner, 234
This Must Be Love Valentine's Day Dinner, 210

Desserts
Baklava with Fruit Compote, 121
Banana Custard, 80
Blueberry Peach Crisp, 134
Buttermilk Chocolate Drops, 24
Cheery Cherry Parfaits, 46
Cliffhanger Cappuccino Coolers, 30
Epilogue Praline-Apple Crisp, 35
Fourth Quarter Chocolate Cheesecake, 208
Golf Ball Cookies, 13
Key Lime Yogurt Pie, 94
Lemon Cake with Brandied Blueberry Sauce, 196–197
Made in Heaven Strawberry Mousse, 219
Minted Melon Balls, 23
No-Bake Cookies, 184
Pears Hélène, 242
pound cake, 108
praline, 35
Pumpkin Mousse, 161
Round 'Em Up Oatmeal Carrot Bars, 57
Scrumptious Carrot Cake, 172–173
Summer Strawberry Shortcake, 108

Dilled Carrots, 230
Dilled Salmon Mousse, 100

Dips
Blue Ribbon Sun-Dried Tomato Dip, 126
Caramel Dipping Sauce, 127
Corn, Onion, Red Pepper, White Bean, and Cilantro Salsa, 86
Cucumber Yogurt Dip, 115
Green Chile Artichoke Dip, 190
Pineapple, Peach, and Jalapeño Salsa, 87
Red, Yellow, and Green Dip with Parmesan Pita Triangles, 62
Spicy Salsa Dip, 50
Three Bean Creole Dip, 166
See also Dressings

Dressings
Fruits of Love Salad with Blushed Vinaigrette, 215
Green Salad with Edible Flowers and Mustard Vinaigrette, 20
Homemade Lemon Dressing, 12
See also Dips

Drinks
alcoholic, and cancer prevention, 245–246
Bloody Mary Mix, 5
Blue Storm, 191
Cherry Limeade, 42
Cliffhanger Cappuccino Coolers, 30
Energizing Smoothie, 140
Flip Juice, 168
green tea, 116
Hot Cocoa, 179
Hot Spiced Cider, 156
Iced Cappuccino, 225
Iced Turkish Coffee, 237
Lemon Watermelon Slush, 68
Montego Bay Papaya Punch, 75
Mulled Punch, 128
Nectar of the Gods, 116
Raspberry Lemonade, 19
Root Beer Floats, 52
Sangria Blanca Punch, 88
Seaside Punch, 63
Sparkling Sunset Citrus Spritzer, 142
Spiced Ginger Tea, 203
Summer Sparkler, 103
Tiramisu, 231
Valentine Spritzers, 214

E

Eggplant
Eggplant Pizza, 171
Grilled Vegetables, 228

Eggs
Breakfast Burritos, 145–146
Farm-Fresh Deviled Eggs, 129
Fourth Quarter Chocolate Cheesecake, 208
Rise 'n Shine English Muffins, 143–144
substitutes, 145–146

Energizing Smoothie, 140

Entertaining
and buffets, v–vi
and creativity, vi
Fall/Winter parties, 123–244
and low fat foods, vi
outdoor, vi
Spring/Summer parties, 1–122
Epilogue Praline-Apple Crisp, 35
Espresso. *See* Coffee
Exercise, 245–246

F

Falafel, 236
Fall/Winter parties
Country Fair Canning Party, 123–136
Game Night, 163–174
Partito Italiano, 221–232
Post-Holiday Blues Party, 187–198
Pre-Hike Breakfast, 137–150
Pumpkin-Carving Contest, 151–162
Season's Greetings Holiday Affair, 175–186
"Souper" Bowl Bash, 199–208
Taste of Nations Dinner, 233–244
This Must Be Love Valentine's Day Dinner, 209–220
Farm-Fresh Deviled Eggs, 129
Fat, vi
Festive Tuna Roll-Ups, 183
Fish. *See* Seafood
Flip Juice, 168
Flowers, edible, 20
Fourth Quarter Chocolate Cheesecake, 208
Fruits
apples, 35, 121, 127, 142
apricots, 128, 157–158, 168
Baklava with Fruit Compote, 121
bananas, 79, 80, 140
blueberries, 134, 194, 196–197
and cancer prevention, 245
cantaloupes, 23, 141
cherries, 42–43, 46, 63
coconuts, 13, 76, 180
cranberries, 43, 63, 156, 168, 214
and edible flowers, 20
Glorious Fruit Salad, 141
grapes, 88, 141, 167, 180
grapefruits, 215
guava, 75
kiwi, 79, 141
lemons, 12, 19, 68, 80, 116–117, 156, 196–197
limes, 94, 141, 168
Make-Your-Own Cereal and On-the-Trail Mix, 148
mango, 79
melons, 23
Mixed Greens with Assorted Vegetables, Fruits, Cheese, and Other Toppings, 11
Mulled Punch, 128
oranges, 21, 31, 103, 130, 142, 156, 191, 203
papayas, 75, 77, 191
passion, 88
peaches, 87, 134
pears, 242
pineapples, 63–64, 79, 87–88, 103, 168, 172–173, 180, 191
raspberries, 19, 74, 192, 214
"Snow"-Dusted Fruit, 180
strawberries, 103, 108, 140, 141, 215, 219
Summer Fruit Salad with Poppy Seed Dressing, 66
tangerines, 142
Tropical Fruit Display, 79
watermelons, 23, 68
zest, 130
See also Appetizers; Salads; Vegetables
Fruits of Love Salad with Blushed Vinaigrette, 215
"Full" House Salad, 169

G

Game Night
activities, 165
decorations, 164
Eggplant Pizza, 171
Flip Juice, 168
"Full" House Salad, 169
Game Piece Grapes, 167
invitations, 164
Scrumptious Carrot Cake, 172–173
setting the scene, 165
Three Bean Creole Dip, 166
Turkey Reuben Grilled Sandwiches, 170

Game Piece Grapes, 167
Get Your Hands Dirty Garden Party
activities, 17
Buttermilk Chocolate Drops, 24
Chilled Asparagus with Horseradish-Dill Dipping Sauce, 18
Curried Chicken Salad, 21
decorations, 16–17
Green Salad with Edible Flowers and Mustard Vinaigrette, 20
invitations, 16
Marinated Artichoke and Potato Salad, 22
Raspberry Lemonade, 19
setting the scene, 17
Ginger Shredded Pork, 8
Glorious Fruit Salad, 141
Golf Ball Cookies, 13
Granola, 184
Grapefruits, 215
Grapes
Game Piece Grapes, 167
Glorious Fruit Salad, 141
Sangría Blanca Punch, 88
"Snow"-Dusted Fruit, 180
Greek Chicken with Tomatoes, Peppers, Olives, and Feta, 118
Greek Salad, 120
Greek Zucchini, 241
Green Chile Artichoke Dip, 190
Green Salad with Edible Flowers and Mustard Vinaigrette, 20
Greens, mixed, 11
Grenadine, 142
Grilled Portabella Mushrooms, 10
Grilled Vegetables, 228
Grilling
Chianti-Grilled Mushrooms and Onions, 224
Grilled Vegetables, 228
Lemon Barbecued Shrimp, 7
skewers and, 7
Texas Dry-Rub Barbecue, 54
Guava, 75

H

Halfback Beef Burgundy Soup, 206
Harvest Ham Primavera, 132–133
Harvest Rice, 160
Hearty Veggie Alphabet Soup, 181
Heavenly Hummus, 114
Herb-Rubbed Pork Loin with Apricot-Pecan Stuffing, 157–158
Herbs and spices
allspice, 77, 128, 156, 161
basil, 4, 28–29, 126, 169, 207, 229
chives, 28–29, 32, 132–133, 167
cilantro, 86, 89–91, 93, 105–106, 205
cinnamon, 156, 161, 179, 208, 225
cloves, 93, 203
dill, 100, 230, 240
fennel, 218, 228
garlic, 195, 217, 224, 227, 229, 236, 238, 241
ginger, 8, 77, 156, 203
mint, 119, 141
nutmeg, 161, 179, 191
oregano, 62, 67, 115, 120
paprika, 240
parsley, 28–29, 101–102, 115
rosemary, 28–29, 227
Texas Dry-Rub Barbecue, 54
Home on the Range Hoedown
activities, 49
Cowboy Cornbread, 51
decorations, 48
invitations, 48
Ranch Beans, 53
Root Beer Floats, 52
Round 'Em Up Oatmeal Carrot Bars, 57
setting the scene, 49
Spicy Salsa Dip, 50
Texas Dry-Rub Barbecue, 54
Tri-Colored Jalapeño Slaw, 55
Homemade Lemon Dressing, 12
Hot Cocoa, 179
Hot Spiced Cider, 156
Hummus, 114
Hungarian Chicken, 240

I

"I Got the Blues" Chicken, 193
Iced Cappuccino, 225
Iced Turkish Coffee, 237
Indian Curried Carrot Soup, 239
Invitations

Backyard Beach Barbecue, 60
Book Club Supper, 26
Country Fair Canning Party, 124
Croquet Classic, 98
Game Night, 164
Get Your Hands Dirty Garden Party, 16
Home on the Range Hoedown, 48
Jamaican Jam, 72
Life is a Bowl of Cherries Celebration, 38
Mount Olympus Greek Party, 112
On the "Green" Golf Party, 2
Partito Italiano, 222
Post-Holiday Blues Party, 188
Pre-Hike Breakfast, 138
Pumpkin-Carving Contest, 152
Salsa Party, 84
Season's Greetings Holiday Affair, 176
"Souper" Bowl Bash, 200
Taste of Nations Dinner, 234
This Must Be Love Valentine's Day Dinner, 210

J

Jalapeños
Breakfast Burritos, 145–146
Green Chile Artichoke Dip, 190
Pineapple, Peach, and Jalapeño Salsa, 87
Tri-Colored Jalapeño Slaw, 55
Jamaican Jam
activities, 73
Baked Sweet Potato Wedges, 78
Banana Custard, 80
Black Beans and Rice with Papaya and Red Onions, 77
Coconut-Rum Salmon, 76
decorations, 72
invitations, 72
Jerk Shrimp with Berry Sauce, 74
Montego Bay Papaya Punch, 75
setting the scene, 73
Tropical Fruit Display, 79
Jerk Shrimp with Berry Sauce, 74
Jicama Slaw, 92
Julienned Carrot and Celery Orzo, 104

K

Key Lime Yogurt Pie, 94
Kick-Off Crunch, 202
Kiwi, 79, 141

L

Lemon Barbecued Shrimp, 7
Lemon Cake with Brandied Blueberry Sauce, 196–197
Lemon Spinach Soup, 117
Lemon Watermelon Slush, 68
Lemons
Banana Custard, 80
Homemade Lemon Dressing, 12
Hot Spiced Cider, 156
Lemon Barbecued Shrimp, 7
Lemon Cake with Brandied Blueberry Sauce, 196–197
Lemon Spinach Soup, 117
Lemon Watermelon Slush, 68
Nectar of the Gods, 116
Raspberry Lemonade, 19
Life is a Bowl of Cherries Celebration
activities, 39
Brown Rice Pilaf, 45
Cheery Cherry Parfaits, 46
Cherry Limeade, 42
Crispy Shrimp Sensations, 41
Crunchy Green Beans with Caramelized Onions, 44
decorations, 38
invitations, 38
Roast Turkey Breast with Sour Cherry Sauce, 43
setting the scene, 39
Zucchini Bites, 40
Limes
Flip Juice, 168
Glorious Fruit Salad, 141
Key Lime Yogurt Pie, 94
Linguini with Tomato, Basil, and Capers, 229
Low-fat foods, 245

M

Made in Heaven Strawberry Mousse, 219
Main dishes
Coconut-Rum Salmon, 76
Eggplant Pizza, 171
Festive Tuna Roll-Ups, 183
Ginger Shredded Pork, 8
Greek Chicken with Tomatoes, Peppers, Olives, and Feta, 118
Harvest Ham Primavera, 132–133
Herb-Rubbed Pork Loin with Apricot-Pecan Stuffing, 157–158
Hungarian Chicken, 240
"I Got the Blues" Chicken, 193
Lemon Barbecued Shrimp, 7
Linguini with Tomato, Basil, and Capers, 229
Page-Turner Tuna Steaks with Ginger-Lime Crust, 33
Roast Turkey Breast with Sour Cherry Sauce, 43
Rosemary Beef with Shallot Sauce, 216
Skewered Shrimp, Chicken, and Pineapple with Honey Orange Dipping Sauce, 64
Spiced Chicken Breast, 6
Texas Dry-Rub Barbecue, 54
Turkey Reuben Grilled Sandwiches, 170
See also Salads; Side dishes
Make-Your-Own Cereal and On-the-Trail Mix, 148
Mango, 79
Marinated Artichoke and Potato Salad, 22
Marshmallows, 179
Meat. *See* Beef
Melons, 23
Mexican Chicken Salad, 89
Middle Eastern Baked Falafel, 236
Mini Bean Croquettes with Tomato-Anchovy Dip, 101–102
Minted Melon Balls, 23
Mixed Greens with Assorted Vegetables, Fruits, Cheese, and Other Toppings, 11
Mixed Greens with Berry-Mustard Vinaigrette, 192
Montego Bay Papaya Punch, 75
Mount Olympus Greek Party
activities, 113
Baklava with Fruit Compote, 121
Cucumber Yogurt Dip, 115
decorations, 112
Greek Chicken with Tomatoes, Peppers, Olives, and Feta, 118
Greek Salad, 120
Heavenly Hummus, 114
invitations, 112
Lemon Spinach Soup, 117
Nectar of the Gods, 116
Rice with Orzo and Mint, 119
setting the scene, 113
Mulled Punch, 128
Mushrooms
Artichoke Hearts Toscana, 238
Chianti-Grilled Mushrooms and Onions, 224
Grilled Portabella Mushrooms, 10
Hungarian Chicken, 240
"I Got the Blues" Chicken, 193
Rise 'n Shine English Muffins, 143–144
Rosemary Beef with Shallot Sauce, 216

N

Nectar of the Gods, 116
No-Bake Cookies, 184
Novel New Potatoes and Sugar Snap Peas, 34
Nutrition
and cancer prevention, 245–246
and conversion tables for cooking, 248
resources, 246–247
Nuts and seeds, 11
almonds, 194
Baklava with Fruit Compote, 121
Game Piece Grapes, 167
Herb-Rubbed Pork Loin with Apricot-Pecan Stuffing, 157–158
Make-Your-Own Cereal and On-the-Trail Mix, 148
No-Bake Cookies, 184
Summer Fruit Salad with Poppy Seed Dressing, 66

O

Oatmeal, 57
Olives

Antipasto Salad, 226
Greek Chicken with Tomatoes, Peppers, Olives, and Feta, 118
Greek Salad, 120
Polenta Hearts with Roasted Red Pepper and Olive Tapenade, 212–213
On the "Green" Golf Party
activities, 3
Basil and Tomato Bruschetta, 4
Black Bean Cakes, 9
Bloody Mary Mix, 5
decorations, 2
Ginger Shredded Pork, 8
Golf Ball Cookies, 13
Grilled Portabella Mushrooms, 10
Homemade Lemon Dressing, 12
invitations, 2
Lemon Barbecued Shrimp, 7
Mixed Greens with Assorted Vegetables, Fruits, Cheese, and Other Toppings, 11
setting the scene, 3
Spiced Chicken Breast, 6
Onions
Artichoke Hearts Toscana, 238
Black Bean-Filled Sweet Potato Biscuits with Queso Fresco, 90–91
Black Beans and Rice with Papaya and Red Onions, 77
Breakfast Burritos, 145–146
Brown Rice Pilaf, 45
Caribbean Rice and Beans, 93
Chianti-Grilled Mushrooms and Onions, 224
Corn, Onion, Red Pepper, White Bean, and Cilantro Salsa, 86
Creamy Double-O Relish, 130
Crunchy Green Beans with Caramelized Onions, 44
Fruits of Love Salad with Blushed Vinaigrette, 215
"Full" House Salad, 169
Greek Zucchini, 241
Halfback Beef Burgundy Soup, 206
Hearty Veggie Alphabet Soup, 181
Herb-Rubbed Pork Loin with Apricot-Pecan Stuffing, 157–158
Hungarian Chicken, 240
Indian Curried Carrot Soup, 239
Lemon Spinach Soup, 117
Linguini with Tomato, Basil, and Capers, 229
Middle Eastern Baked Falafel, 236
Ranch Beans, 53
Sideline Chicken Chili, 205
Spinach Soufflé, 159
Three Bean Creole Dip, 166
Touchdown Tomato-Basil Soup, 207
Turkey Sausage Bites with Sweet Hot Mustard Sauce, 155
White Bean Salad, 67
Zucchini and Squash Tart, 107
Oranges
Best-Seller Beet and Orange Salad, 31
Blue Storm, 191
Creamy Double-O Relish, 130
Curried Chicken Salad, 21
Hot Spiced Cider, 156
Sparkling Sunset Citrus Spritzer, 142
Spiced Ginger Tea, 203
Summer Sparkler, 103
Orzo
Julienned Carrot and Celery Orzo, 104
Rice with Orzo and Mint, 119

P

Page-Turner Tuna Steaks with Ginger-Lime Crust, 33
Papayas
Black Beans and Rice with Papaya and Red Onions, 77
Blue Storm, 191
Montego Bay Papaya Punch, 75
Tropical Fruit Display, 79
Parboiling, 18
Partito Italiano
activities, 223
Antipasto Salad, 226
Chianti-Grilled Mushrooms and Onions, 224
decorations, 222
Dilled Carrots, 230
Grilled Vegetables, 228
Iced Cappuccino, 225
invitations, 222
Linguini with Tomato, Basil, and Capers, 229
setting the scene, 223

Tiramisu, 231
Passion fruits, 88
Pasta
Harvest Ham Primavera, 132–133
Hungarian Chicken, 240
Linguini with Tomato, Basil, and Capers, 229
Peaches
Blueberry Peach Crisp, 134
Pineapple, Peach, and Jalapeño Salsa, 87
Pears Hélène, 242
Peas
Harvest Ham Primavera, 132–133
Novel New Potatoes and Sugar Snap Peas, 34
Pepperoni, 226
Peppers
Antipasto Salad, 226
Black Bean Cakes, 9
Caribbean Rice and Beans, 93
Corn, Onion, Red Pepper, White Bean, and Cilantro Salsa, 86
Greek Chicken with Tomatoes, Peppers, Olives, and Feta, 118
Greek Salad, 120
Grilled Vegetables, 228
Harvest Ham Primavera, 132–133
Indian Curried Carrot Soup, 239
Jicama Slaw, 92
Mexican Chicken Salad, 89
Polenta Hearts with Roasted Red Pepper and Olive Tapenade, 212–213
"Read" Pepper Soup with Sour Cream and Chives, 32
Red Bliss Potato Salad, 65
Red, Yellow, and Green Dip with Parmesan Pita Triangles, 62
Rise 'n Shine English Muffins, 143–144
Rosemary Beef with Shallot Sauce, 216
Seared Sesame Scallops with Avocado Sauce, 105–106
Three Bean Creole Dip, 166
Turkey Sausage Bites with Sweet Hot Mustard Sauce, 155
Pineapple, Peach, and Jalapeño Salsa, 87
Pineapples
Blue Storm, 191
Flip Juice, 168
Pineapple, Peach, and Jalapeño Salsa, 87
Sangría Blanca Punch, 88
Scrumptious Carrot Cake, 172–173
Seaside Punch, 63
Skewered Shrimp, Chicken, and Pineapple with Honey Orange Dipping Sauce, 64
"Snow"-Dusted Fruit, 180
Summer Sparkler, 103
Tropical Fruit Display, 79
Pita bread
Heavenly Hummus, 114
Red, Yellow, and Green Dip with Parmesan Pita Triangles, 62
Polenta Hearts with Roasted Red Pepper and Olive Tapenade, 212–213
Pork
Ginger Shredded Pork, 8
Harvest Ham Primavera, 132–133
Herb-Rubbed Pork Loin with Apricot-Pecan Stuffing, 157–158
Post-Holiday Blues Party
activities, 189
Blue Storm, 191
Couscous with Almonds, Dried Blueberries, and Parmesan Cheese, 194
decorations, 188
Green Chile Artichoke Dip, 190
"I Got the Blues" Chicken, 193
invitations, 188
Lemon Cake with Brandied Blueberry Sauce, 196–197
Mixed Greens with Berry-Mustard Vinaigrette, 192
Roasted Garlicky Potatoes, 195
setting the scene, 189
Potatoes
Baked Sweet Potato Wedges, 78
Black Bean-Filled Sweet Potato Biscuits with Queso Fresco, 90–91
Buttermilk Garlic Mashed Potatoes, 217
Marinated Artichoke and Potato Salad, 22
Novel New Potatoes and Sugar Snap Peas, 34
"Read" Pepper Soup with Sour Cream and Chives, 32
Red Bliss Potato Salad, 65
Roasted Garlicky Potatoes, 195
Poultry. *See* Chicken
Pound cake, 108
Pralines, 35

Pre-Hike Breakfast
activities, 139
Breakfast Burritos, 145–146
decorations, 138
Energizing Smoothie, 140
Glorious Fruit Salad, 141
invitations, 138
Make-Your-Own Cereal and On-the-Trail Mix, 148
Pumpkin Oat Muffins, 147
Rise 'n Shine English Muffins, 143–144
setting the scene, 139
Sparkling Sunset Citrus Spritzer, 142
Pumpkin-Carving Contest
activities, 153
decorations, 152
Harvest Rice, 160
Herb-Rubbed Pork Loin with Apricot-Pecan Stuffing, 157–158
Hot Spiced Cider, 156
invitations, 152
Pumpkin Mousse, 161
Scary Spiced Popcorn, 154
setting the scene, 153
Spinach Soufflé, 159
Turkey Sausage Bites with Sweet Hot Mustard Sauce, 155
Pumpkin Mousse, 161
Pumpkin Oat Muffins, 147

R

Ranch Beans, 53
Raspberries
Jerk Shrimp with Berry Sauce, 74
Mixed Greens with Berry-Mustard Vinaigrette, 192
Raspberry Lemonade, 19
Valentine Spritzers, 214
"Read" Pepper Soup with Sour Cream and Chives, 32
Red Bliss Potato Salad, 65
Red, Yellow, and Green Dip with Parmesan Pita Triangles, 62
Resources for nutrition promotion, 246–247
Rice
Black Beans and Rice with Papaya and Red Onions, 77
Brown Rice Pilaf, 45
Caribbean Rice and Beans, 93
Confetti Beans and Rice, 182
Harvest Rice, 160
Herb-Rubbed Pork Loin with Apricot-Pecan Stuffing, 157–158
Rice with Orzo and Mint, 119
Rice with Orzo and Mint, 119
Rise 'n Shine English Muffins, 143–144
Roast Turkey Breast with Sour Cherry Sauce, 43
Roasted Garlicky Potatoes, 195
Root Beer Floats, 52
Rosemary Beef with Shallot Sauce, 216
Roses, 20
Round 'Em Up Oatmeal Carrot Bars, 57
Ruby Red Beets with Fennel, 218

S

Salads
Antipasto Salad, 226
Best-Seller Beet and Orange Salad, 31
Caesar Salad, 204
Country Coleslaw, 131
Curried Chicken Salad, 21
and edible flowers, 20
Fruits of Love Salad with Blushed Vinaigrette, 215
"Full" House Salad, 169
Glorious Fruit Salad, 141
Greek Salad, 120
Green Salad with Edible Flowers and Mustard Vinaigrette, 20
Marinated Artichoke and Potato Salad, 22
Mexican Chicken Salad, 89
Mixed Greens with Assorted Vegetables, Fruits, Cheese, and Other Toppings, 11
Mixed Greens with Berry-Mustard Vinaigrette, 192
Red Bliss Potato Salad, 65
Summer Fruit Salad with Poppy Seed Dressing, 66
Tri-Colored Jalapeño Slaw, 55
White Bean Salad, 67
See also Appetizers; Fruits; Main dishes; Side dishes; Vegetables
Salami, 226
Salsa Party

activities, 85
Black Bean-Filled Sweet Potato Biscuits with Queso Fresco, 90–91
Caribbean Rice and Beans, 93
Corn, Onion, Red Pepper, White Bean, and Cilantro Salsa, 86
decorations, 84
invitations, 84
Jicama Slaw, 92
Key Lime Yogurt Pie, 94
Mexican Chicken Salad, 89
Pineapple, Peach, and Jalapeño Salsa, 87
Sangría Blanca Punch, 88
setting the scene, 85
Sangría Blanca Punch, 88
Scary Spiced Popcorn, 154
Scrumptious Carrot Cake, 172–173
Seafood
anchovies, 101–102
and cancer prevention, 245
Coconut-Rum Salmon, 76
Crispy Shrimp Sensations, 41
Dilled Salmon Mousse, 100
Festive Tuna Roll-Ups, 183
Lemon Barbecued Shrimp, 7
Page-Turner Tuna Steaks with Ginger-Lime Crust, 33
salmon, 76, 100
scallops, 105–106
Seared Sesame Scallops with Avocado Sauce, 105–106
shrimp, 7, 41
tuna, 7, 33, 183
Seared Sesame Scallops with Avocado Sauce, 105–106
Seaside Punch, 63
Season's Greetings Holiday Affair
activities, 176–177
Confetti Beans and Rice, 182
decorations, 176
Festive Tuna Roll-Ups, 183
Hearty Veggie Alphabet Soup, 181
Hot Cocoa, 179
invitations, 176
No-Bake Cookies, 184
setting the scene, 177
"Snow"-Dusted Fruit, 180
Spinach and Tomato Quesadilla Trees, 178
Setting the scene
Backyard Beach Barbecue, 61
Book Club Supper, 27
Country Fair Canning Party, 125
Croquet Classic, 99
Game Night, 165
Get Your Hands Dirty Garden Party, 17
Home on the Range Hoedown, 49
Jamaican Jam, 73
Life is a Bowl of Cherries Celebration, 39
Mount Olympus Greek Party, 113
On the "Green" Golf Party, 3
Partito Italiano, 223
Post-Holiday Blues Party, 189
Pre-Hike Breakfast, 139
Pumpkin-Carving Contest, 153
Salsa Party, 85
Season's Greetings Holiday Affair, 177
"Souper" Bowl Bash, 201
Taste of Nations Dinner, 235
This Must Be Love Valentine's Day Dinner, 211
Shallots, 216
Shellfish. *See* Seafood
Shrimp
Crispy Shrimp Sensations, 41
Jerk Shrimp with Berry Sauce, 74
Lemon Barbecued Shrimp, 7
Skewered Shrimp, Chicken, and Pineapple with Honey Orange Dipping Sauce, 64
See also Seafood
Side dishes
Artichoke Hearts Toscana, 238
Baked Sweet Potato Wedges, 78
Black Bean Cakes, 9
Black Bean-Filled Sweet Potato Biscuits with Queso Fresco, 90–91
Black Beans and Rice with Papaya and Red Onions, 77
Brown Rice Pilaf, 45
Buttermilk Garlic Mashed Potatoes, 217
Caribbean Rice and Beans, 93
Chilled Asparagus with Horseradish-Dill Dipping Sauce, 18
Confetti Beans and Rice, 182
Couscous with Almonds, Dried Blueberries, and Parmesan Cheese, 194

Crunchy Green Beans with Caramelized Onions, 44
Dilled Carrots, 230
Farm-Fresh Deviled Eggs, 129
Greek Zucchini, 241
Grilled Portabella Mushrooms, 10
Grilled Vegetables, 228
Harvest Rice, 160
Jicama Slaw, 92
Julienned Carrot and Celery Orzo, 104
Middle Eastern Baked Falafel, 236
Novel New Potatoes and Sugar Snap Peas, 34
Polenta Hearts with Roasted Red Pepper and Olive Tapenade, 212–213
Ranch Beans, 53
Red Bliss Potato Salad, 65
Rice with Orzo and Mint, 119
Roasted Garlicky Potatoes, 195
Ruby Red Beets with Fennel, 218
Seared Sesame Scallops with Avocado Sauce, 105–106
Spinach Soufflé, 159
Zucchini and Squash Tart, 107
See also Breads and grains; Main dishes
Sideline Chicken Chili, 205
Skewered Shrimp, Chicken, and Pineapple with Honey Orange Dipping Sauce, 64
Skewers, 7, 64
Smoking and cancer prevention, 246
"Snow"-Dusted Fruit, 180
"Souper" Bowl Bash
activities, 201
Caesar Salad, 204
decorations, 200
Fourth Quarter Chocolate Cheesecake, 208
Halfback Beef Burgundy Soup, 206
invitations, 200
Kick-Off Crunch, 202
setting the scene, 201
Sideline Chicken Chili, 205
Spiced Ginger Tea, 203
Touchdown Tomato-Basil Soup, 207
Soups
Halfback Beef Burgundy Soup, 206
Hearty Veggie Alphabet Soup, 181
Indian Curried Carrot Soup, 239
Lemon Spinach Soup, 117
"Read" Pepper Soup with Sour Cream and Chives, 32
Touchdown Tomato-Basil Soup, 207
Soy, 140
Sparkling Sunset Citrus Spritzer, 142
Spiced Chicken Breast, 6
Spiced Ginger Tea, 203
Spicy Salsa Dip, 50
Spinach
Fruits of Love Salad with Blushed Vinaigrette, 215
Lemon Spinach Soup, 117
Mixed Greens with Berry-Mustard Vinaigrette, 192
Seared Sesame Scallops with Avocado Sauce, 105–106
Spinach and Tomato Quesadilla Trees, 178
Spinach Soufflé, 159
Spinach and Tomato Quesadilla Trees, 178
Spinach Soufflé, 159
Spring/Summer parties
Backyard Beach Barbecue, 59–70
Book Club Supper, 25–36
Croquet Classic, 97–110
Get Your Hands Dirty Garden Party, 15–36
Home on the Range Hoedown, 47–58
Jamaican Jam, 71–82
Life is a Bowl of Cherries Celebration, 37–46
Mount Olympus Greek Party, 111–122
On the "Green" Golf Party, 1–14
Salsa Party, 83–96
Squash
Grilled Vegetables, 228
Zucchini and Squash Tart, 107
Strawberries
Energizing Smoothie, 140
Fruits of Love Salad with Blushed Vinaigrette, 215
Glorious Fruit Salad, 141
Made in Heaven Strawberry Mousse, 219
Summer Sparkler, 103
Summer Strawberry Shortcake, 108
Summer Fruit Salad with Poppy Seed Dressing, 66
Summer Sparkler, 103
Summer Strawberry Shortcake, 108

T

Tabasco, 90–91
Tangerines, 142
Taste of Nations Dinner
  activities, 235
  Artichoke Hearts Toscana, 238
  decorations, 234
  Greek Zucchini, 241
  Hungarian Chicken, 240
  Iced Turkish Coffee, 237
  Indian Curried Carrot Soup, 239
  invitations, 234
  Middle Eastern Baked Falafel, 236
  Pears Hélène, 242
  setting the scene, 235
Texas Dry-Rub Barbecue, 54
Themes
  Backyard Beach Barbecue, 59–70
  Book Club Supper, 25–36
  Country Fair Canning Party, 123–136
  Croquet Classic, 97–110
  Game Night, 163–174
  Get Your Hands Dirty Garden Party, 15–36
  Home on the Range Hoedown, 47–58
  Jamaican Jam, 71–82
  Life is a Bowl of Cherries Celebration, 37–46
  Mount Olympus Greek Party, 111–122
  On the "Green" Golf Party, 1–14
  Partito Italiano, 222–232
  Post-Holiday Blues Party, 187–198
  Pre-Hike Breakfast, 137–150
  Pumpkin-Carving Contest, 151–162
  Salsa Party, 83–96
  Season's Greetings Holiday Affair, 175–186
  "Souper" Bowl Bash, 199–208
  Taste of Nations Dinner, 233–244
  This Must Be Love Valentine's Day Dinner, 209–220
This Must Be Love Valentine's Day Dinner
  activities, 211
  Buttermilk Garlic Mashed Potatoes, 217
  decorations, 210
  Fruits of Love Salad with Blushed Vinaigrette, 215
  invitations, 210
  Made in Heaven Strawberry Mousse, 219
  Polenta Hearts with Roasted Red Pepper and Olive Tapenade, 212–213
  Rosemary Beef with Shallot Sauce, 216
  Ruby Red Beets with Fennel, 218
  setting the scene, 211
  Valentine Spritzers, 214
Three Bean Creole Dip, 166
Tiramisu, 231
Tobacco and cancer, 246
Tofu, 140
Tomatoes
  Antipasto Salad, 226
  Artichoke Hearts Toscana, 238
  Basil and Tomato Bruschetta, 4
  Blue Ribbon Sun-Dried Tomato Dip, 126
  Caribbean Rice and Beans, 93
  Confetti Beans and Rice, 182
  Eggplant Pizza, 171
  "Full" House Salad, 169
  Greek Chicken with Tomatoes, Peppers, Olives, and Feta, 118
  Greek Zucchini, 241
  Linguini with Tomato, Basil, and Capers, 229
  Polenta Hearts with Roasted Red Pepper and Olive Tapenade, 212–213
  Red, Yellow, and Green Dip with Parmesan Pita Triangles, 62
  Spinach and Tomato Quesadilla Trees, 178
  Three Bean Creole Dip, 166
  Touchdown Tomato-Basil Soup, 207
  White Bean Salad, 67
Touchdown Tomato-Basil Soup, 207
Tri-Colored Jalapeño Slaw, 55
Tropical Fruit Display, 79
Turkey
  Roast Turkey Breast with Sour Cherry Sauce, 43
  Turkey Reuben Grilled Sandwiches, 170
  Turkey Sausage Bites with Sweet Hot Mustard Sauce, 155
  See also Chicken
Turkey Reuben Grilled Sandwiches, 170
Turkey Sausage Bites with Sweet Hot Mustard Sauce, 155

U

U.S. Department of Agriculture, 247

V

Valentine Spritzers, 214
Vegetables
- artichokes, 22, 171, 190, 226, 238
- asparagus, 18
- avocados, 105–106
- beets, 31, 206, 218
- blanching, 18
- cabbage, 55, 92, 131
- carrots, 55, 57, 90–91, 104, 160, 172–173, 181, 229, 230, 239
- celery, 5, 65, 93, 100, 104, 157–158, 229
- chickpeas, 101–102, 114, 226, 236
- chiles, 190, 205
- corn, 51, 86, 181, 190, 205, 226
- cucumbers, 115, 120
- and edible flowers, 20
- eggplant, 171, 228
- fennel, 218, 228
- *Grilled Vegetables*, 228
- jalapeño pepper, 55, 87, 190
- jicama, 92
- melons, 23
- *Mixed Greens with Assorted Vegetables, Fruits, Cheese, and Other Toppings*, 11
- mushrooms, 10, 143–144, 193, 216, 224, 238, 240
- olives, 118, 120, 212–213, 226
- onions, 44–45, 53, 67, 77, 86, 90–91, 93, 117, 130, 145–146, 155, 157–158, 159, 166, 169, 181, 205–207, 215, 224, 229, 236, 238–241
- peas, 34, 132–133
- peppers, 9, 32, 62, 65, 86, 93, 105–106, 120, 132–133, 143–144, 155, 166, 212–213, 226, 228, 239
- potatoes, 22, 32, 34, 65, 195, 217
- pumpkin, 147
- shallots, 216
- spinach, 105–106, 117, 159, 178, 192, 215
- squash, 107, 228
- tomatoes, 4, 62, 93, 126, 166, 169, 171, 178, 182, 207, 212–213, 226, 229, 238, 241
- zucchini, 40, 107, 228, 241
- *Zucchini Bites*, 40
- see also Appetizers; Beans; Fruits; Salads

W

Watermelons
- *Lemon Watermelon Slush*, 68
- *Minted Melon Balls*, 23

White Bean Salad, 67

Y

Yams
- *Baked Sweet Potato Wedges*, 78
- *Black Bean-Filled Sweet Potato Biscuits with Queso Fresco*, 90–91

Yogurt
- *Banana Custard*, 80
- *Cucumber Yogurt Dip*, 115
- *Dilled Salmon Mousse*, 100
- *Energizing Smoothie*, 140
- *Fourth Quarter Chocolate Cheesecake*, 208
- *Heavenly Hummus*, 114
- *Hungarian Chicken*, 240
- *Key Lime Yogurt Pie*, 94
- *Pears Hélène*, 242
- *Summer Fruit Salad with Poppy Seed Dressing*, 66

Z

Zest, 130
Zucchini and Squash Tart, 107
Zucchini
- *Greek Zucchini*, 241
- *Grilled Vegetables*, 228
- *Zucchini and Squash Tart*, 107
- *Zucchini Bites*, 40

Other cookbooks published by the American Cancer Society

American Cancer Society's Healthy Eating Cookbook: A celebration of food, friends, and healthy living, Third Edition

Kids' First Cookbook: Delicious-Nutritious Treats to Make Yourself!

Also published by the American Cancer Society

A Breast Cancer Journey: Your Personal Guidebook, Second Edition

American Cancer Society Consumers Guide to Cancer Drugs, Second Edition, Wilkes and Ades

American Cancer Society's Complementary and Alternative Cancer Methods Handbook

American Cancer Society's Complete Guide to Prostate Cancer, Bostwick et al.

American Cancer Society's Guide to Pain Control: Understanding and Managing Cancer Pain, Revised Edition

Angels & Monsters: A child's eye view of cancer, Murray and Howard

Because...Someone I Love Has Cancer: Kids' Activity Book

Cancer in the Family: Helping Children Cope with a Parent's Illness, Heiney et al.

Cancer: What Causes It, What Doesn't

Caregiving: A Step-By-Step Resource for Caring for the Person with Cancer at Home, Revised Edition, Houts and Bucher

Coming to Terms with Cancer: A Glossary of Cancer-Related Terms, Laughlin

Couples Confronting Cancer: Keeping Your Relationship Strong, Fincannon and Bruss

Crossing Divides: A Couple's Story of Cancer, Hope, and Hiking Montana's Continental Divide, Bischke

Eating Well, Staying Well During and After Cancer, Bloch et al.

Good for You! Reducing Your Risk of Developing Cancer

Healthy Me: A Read-along Coloring & Activity Book, Hawthorne (illustrated by Blyth)

Informed Decisions: The Complete Book of Cancer Diagnosis, Treatment, and Recovery, Second Edition, Eyre, Lange, and Morris

Kicking Butts: Quit Smoking and Take Charge of Your Health

Our Mom Has Cancer, Ackermann and Ackermann

When the Focus Is on Care: Palliative Care and Cancer, Foley et al.